FIRST
INSIGHTS
—— into ——
BUSINESS

Sue Robbins

STUDENTS' BOOK

Longman

Contents

1 *Customers*

In this unit:

- **Language Focus**
  Direct and indirect question forms
  Pronunciation: weak and strong forms /djə/ /du:/

- **Skills**
  Writing: formal letter-writing, capital letters
  Reading: Kwik-Fit advertisement
  Listening: customer service

- **Vocabulary**
  Word partners

- **Business Communication**
  Making offers

Key Vocabulary

▭ 1.1 Companies need **customers**. Some companies provide **goods** such as clothes, cars and food. Other companies provide **services**, for example insurance, banking, information technology or training.

Companies want **repeat business**, in other words, they want customers to buy from them again and again. To win **customer loyalty**, many companies have a **code of practice**, or set of rules, for **customer care**. The code of practice explains what the customer can expect of the company. Customers can complain about the **service**, or help, they receive and the goods they buy.

Lead-in

Read the texts produced by three different companies and answer the questions.

1 What does each company offer the customer?

2 What other examples of good customer care can you think of?

①

BRITISH Airways employees who make customers unhappy must apologise in person. The company also has a number of items that it can give to customers who are dissatisfied with their service. These range from food hampers and calculators to soft toys and chocolates.

②

First Direct is the UK's leading 24 hour personal telephone bank. Our personal service lets you take care of all your banking needs by telephone, at a time and place to suit you, 24 hours a day, 365 days a year.
You can call to check your balance, pay a bill, discuss a personal loan or increase your Visa Card limit. All calls from within the UK are charged at local rates.

③

The IKEA Business Service Package

IKEA Business offers a full range of services to professional customers, companies and organisations. Our trained staff can help with everything from individual workstations, to planning a complete office. As an IKEA Business customer you can purchase from the specialist Business Catalogue, or from the complete range in the store. Optional delivery and assembly services are available on request. Enquire at the store for more details.

Cross-cultural Comparison

1 Attitudes to customer care may be different in different countries. Work in pairs and discuss the five situations below.

WHAT MAKES GOOD CUSTOMER CARE?

A = Excellent   **B** = Good   **C** = Fair   **D** = Poor

Situation 1	A customer waits in a queue for ten minutes.	A B C D
Situation 2	The phone rings eight times before someone in the company answers it.	A B C D
Situation 3	A customer phones a company. The person who answers does not have the information to answer the customer's question, but tries to answer it.	A B C D
Situation 4	A company answers customers' letters in five working days.	A B C D
Situation 5	A customer makes a complaint. The company employee takes all the details, apologises and promises to take action.	A B C D

2 ▭ 1.2 Listen to a man talking about customer care. Which of the situations is he describing? Does he think this is good customer care? What do you think?

Language Focus

Direct and indirect question forms

1 🔲 **1.3 Tim Saunders wants to join a health and fitness club. He phones Hi-tone Health and Fitness Centre. Listen and answer the questions.**

1 What is good about the customer service Tim Saunders receives?

2 Do you have any criticisms of the customer service?

Tim Saunders

2 🔲 **1.3 Tim Saunders asks two types of questions: direct questions and indirect questions.**

Listen again and tick (✓) the questions he asks.

DIRECT QUESTIONS		INDIRECT QUESTIONS	
Wh/How questions		*Wh/How* questions	
1 a How much does it cost?	☐	**1 b** Could you tell me how much it costs?	☐
2 a What are your opening hours?	☑	**2 b** Could you tell me what your opening hours are?	☐
3 a What's the procedure?	☐	**3 b** Could you tell me what the procedure is?	☑
4 a What qualifications do your instructors have?	☐	**4 b** Could you tell me what qualifications your instructors have?	☑
Yes/No questions (The answer to the questions is *yes* or *no*)		*Yes/No* questions (The answer to the questions is *yes* or *no*)	
5 a Do you have fitness classes as well?	☑	**5 b** Could you tell me if you have fitness classes as well?	☐
6 a Is there a maximum number in each class?	☑	**6 b** Can you tell me if there is a maximum number in each class?	☐
7 a Do you offer an introductory session?	☑	**7 b** Could you tell me if you offer an introductory session?	☐
8 a Is it possible to bring guests?	☐	**8 b** Can you tell me if it's possible to bring guests?	☑

3 Look at the direct and indirect questions again and notice the differences between them.

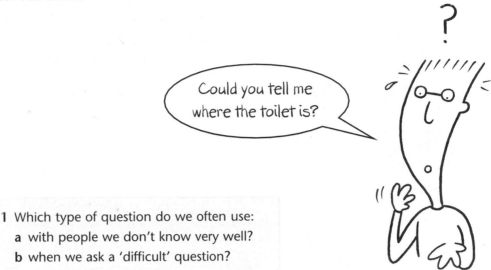

Could you tell me where the toilet is?

1 Which type of question do we often use:
  a with people we don't know very well?
  b when we ask a 'difficult' question?

2 Are the statements below true (T) or false (F)?

Wh/How **questions**

  a For indirect questions we do not use the auxiliary verb *do*.   T/F
  b For indirect questions the main verb comes at the end of the question. T/F

Yes/No **questions**

  c For indirect questions we do not use the auxiliary verb *do*.   T/F
  d For indirect questions we use normal sentence order after the word *if*. T/F

4 In your language do you use different question types for someone you don't know well? How do you change the question?

► **Grammar Reference page 155**

Pronunciation   **Weak and strong forms** /djə/ /duː/

1 ▭ 1.4 Listen to the questions and answers below. Notice the different pronunciation of the verb *do*. Listen again and repeat.

Weak	Strong
1 Do you have fitness classes as well?	Yes, we do.
2 Do you offer an introductory session?	Yes, we do.
3 Do you have a swimming pool?	Yes, we do.
4 Do you have a code of practice?	Yes, we do.

2 When do we use the weak form? When do we use the strong form?

Language Practice

1 Tim Saunders is now at Hi-tone Health and Fitness Centre. The instructor is asking him some questions. Match the two parts of the instructor's questions.

1	Do you	a	do you want to come to the Centre?
2	What are	b	what your objectives are?
3	Could you tell me if	c	you have any medical problems or injuries?
4	How often	d	do any exercise at the moment?
5	Can you tell me	e	your favourite sports?
6	What	f	do you do?

2 Now match Tim Saunders' answers to each question in exercise 1.

Example: **1 d** *Do you do any exercise at the moment?*
        iii *No, I don't. And the problem is I sit at my desk all day.*

6 **i** I'm a business analyst.

5 **ii** I want to get fit and I want to lose a few kilos too.

1 **iii** No, I don't. And the problem is I sit at my desk all day.

4 **iv** Probably three or four times a week.

2 **v** I like swimming and I enjoy a game of squash now and again!

3 **vi** No, I'm very healthy, thank goodness.

3 ☐ 1.5 Now listen and check your answers.

4 Work in pairs. Student A is a customer and Student B is a health club manager.

STUDENT A

You want to join a health and fitness club. You visit a club for an introductory session and meet the manager. You know it is expensive to join – all clubs are – so you want to get a lot of information about the services they offer.

Answer Student B's questions.
Use direct and indirect questions to ask about

- opening hours
- facilities
- fitness classes
- class sizes
- possibility of bringing guests

Now decide if you want to join the club and give your reasons. (Don't say what you decide yet!)

STUDENT B

Welcome the customer. Find out his/her

- name
- job
- fitness level

Answer his/her questions about the club's opening hours and facilities.

When you have finished decide if you think Student A wants to join the club. Give your reasons. Then ask Student A if you are right.

Writing

Capital letters

1 **Read the lists below. When do we use capital letters?**

Example 1: *We use capital letters for people's names and titles.*

1 Dr Yemeh, Ms Perez, Prof. Brown, Sir David, Danuta Lochowski
2 the Customer Service Manager, the Personnel Director
3 Oxford Street, the Champs Elysées
4 London, Paris, Tokyo, New York
5 the River Thames, Mount Etna, the Black Forest
6 Monday, Tuesday, Saturday, April, September, June
7 Christmas Day, Ramadan, New Year
8 Finland, Brazil, Fin, Brazilian, Finnish, Brazilian
9 the Ritz Hotel, the Guggenheim Museum, the British Museum
10 First Direct, BA (British Airways), Coca-Cola
11 a CD, a TV, a BMW, a VW, an XR3i

2 **Read the letter. The writer has problems with his word processor. Where does he need to use capital letters? For more on letter writing, see Workbook page 71.**

Hi-tone

HEALTH AND FITNESS CENTRE

rushmoor hotel, crawley, west sussex
phone/fax: 011293 4000064

20 july

mr t saunders
25 crawley road
reigate

dear mr saunders

we are delighted to enclose your membership card for hi-tone health and fitness centre.
on your next visit one of our instructors will guide you through your new fitness programme and show you how to use the equipment in the gym. please phone to arrange a time convenient to you.
we hope to welcome you to our many social events. we have an action-packed programme over the summer starting with a 1970s disco evening on 4 june.
as a member of the centre you are entitled to a 15% discount on food and drink. The sports bar is also equipped with Sky tv*.
we look forward to seeing you soon.

yours sincerely

Julian Darleston

julian darleston
assistant manager

*Sky TV: a satellite TV station with sports channels

Listening

Customer Service

1 🔊 **1.6a** Listen to Ann Hislop and Stephen Nicholl talking about a bank called First Direct and a multinational retailer called Marks & Spencer.

1 Who is loyal to Marks & Spencer?

a Ann ☐   **b** Stephen ☐   **c** Ann and Stephen ☑

2 Which words do Ann and Stephen use to describe the staff at Marks & Spencer?

a friendly	☑		**e** professional	☑
b courteous	☐		**f** well-dressed	☐
c helpful	☑		**g** co-operative	☑
d quick	☑		**h** loyal to the company	☑

3 Which word does Ann use to describe the quality of the products?

4 How does Stephen do his banking?

a by going to the bank ☐   **b** by phone ☑   **c** by post ☐

2 🔊 **1.6b** Listen again to Stephen's opinion of First Direct. Complete the summary.

> Stephen is ¹ _loyal_ to First Direct because they are extremely
> ² _efficient_. He can do his banking over the ³ _phone_ at any time of
> the day; he can find out how much there is in his ⁴ _account_ and he can
> pay his ⁵ _bill_. He also thinks the staff are very ⁶ _professional_ and
> very ⁷ _friendly_.

3 Work in pairs. Find the opposites to the words in exercise 1, question 2.

```
d i s c o u r t e o u s t h m u
i y a c m n r p l u n k c b v n
s l o w i f b e i m p o l l t c
l a k a d r i f a t r w b a i o
o g e p n i e z o d o l t r a o
y s e n o e s i e c f r e y r p
a c o i d n s o b g e d s n l e
l t d e i d q w q v s o p r t r
b e m o l l m u j d s m b s i a
o y t u c y x z o r i v r e f t
a i o n b k b r o x o e t k n i
s n o a h r n m i t n i c a e v
l d c s u w p n w c a u w s h e
m g u n h e l p f u l e e a o s
b a d l y d r e s s e d h l n w
```

4 Work in pairs. Think of a company and discuss the attitude of the staff and the quality of the products or services.

Reading

1 Kwik-Fit is a company which puts new parts on cars while the customer waits. Scan the advertisement and give reasons for choosing Kwik-Fit.

1 Open _____ days per week.
2 _____
3 Free _____
4 _____ tyre-fitting.
5 Extended _____

2 Here are five benefits that Kwik-Fit offers its customers:

a	long hours	**d**	free service
b	fast service	**e**	peace of mind
c	customer choice		

Read the text carefully and match each benefit to one of the reasons (1–5) in exercise 1.

Example:
a *long hours – 1 Open seven days a week (para 1)*

Vocabulary

Word partners

1 Match the words below to make four word partners from the text.

1	Kwik-Fit	**a**	helpline
2	late night	**b**	guarantee
3	lifelong	**c**	openings
4	customer	**d**	fitter

2 Now use the word partners to complete these sentences.

1 More and more shops have _____ _____ _____ to allow people to shop after work.

2 A _____ _____ on exhausts means Kwik-Fit repairs problems to its own exhaust pipes free of charge.

3 Many companies have a 24 hour _____ _____ so people can phone in for help at any time.

4 The Kwik-Fit slogan is "You can't get better than a _____ _____!".

valve

exhaust

puncture

You can't get better than a Kwik-Fit fitter!

Here are a few reasons why Kwik-Fit should be your first stop on the road to winter safety this year:

OPEN 7 DAYS
Late Night Openings

INDEPENDENCE
You have the freedom to choose what is best for your car and your pocket.

FREE PUNCTURE REPAIR SERVICE
Any car or van tyre repair that can be carried out on our own premises will be done free of charge. You only pay for a new valve and wheel balance if required.

EXPRESS TYRE FITTING
Our Kwik-Fit fitters promise to fit each tyre in under 10 minutes, timed from acceptance of our quotation.

EXTENDED GUARANTEES
Ask about our 'No Quibble' Accidental Damage guarantee on tyres and our 'Lifelong Guarantee' on exhausts.

Free Customer Helpline 0800 75 76 77.

If you do have any comments about our service or our products, tell us and we'll do everything possible to put the matter right.

In this unit:

- **Language Focus**
  Present simple and present continuous
  Pronunciation: third person singular /s/ /z/ /ɪz/,
  sentence stress

- **Skills**
  Writing: avoiding repetition
  Reading: FT Graduate Training Programme
  Listening: four major companies

- **Vocabulary**
  Word building

- **Business Communication**
  Presenting information

Key Vocabulary

2.1 Companies are involved in many activities, for example **buying, selling, marketing** and **production**, in a range of different industries, such as **information technology**, **telecommunications**, **film**, and **car manufacture**. Many well-known companies are **multinationals**, these are companies which **operate** in a number of countries.

Multinationals often have a complicated structure. There is usually a **parent** or **holding company**. This company owns other companies or parts of other companies. These other companies are called **subsidiaries**.

Lead-in

1 Look at the photos and identify the four companies.

http://www.reuters.com/

2 Match the information about these multinational companies to the correct company logo.

Company logo	Company activities	The company says
REUTERS	**1** The third largest record company in the world. It is also the world's largest publisher of songs and music.	**a** *'We are committed to providing high quality food.'*
The EMI Group	**2** The world's largest hamburger restaurant company. It has over 19,000 restaurants in 100 countries.	**b** *'(We) lead the world in the provision of news and financial information to broadcasters, newspapers, financial markets and on-line services.'*
DHL WORLDWIDE EXPRESS®	**3** This company provides news and financial data to the business community.	**c** *'We aim to be the world's premier music company in all aspects of our business.'*
McDonald's	**4** This company is an international air-express carrier. It delivers packages and documents all over the world.	**d** *'We keep your promises.'*

3 Work in groups. Choose three of these companies.

BMW	Coca-Cola	Nike	Levi Strauss & Co.	Microsoft

Write what you know about:
1 what each company produces or provides
2 where the company started
3 where the company operates
4 who its main competitors are

Language Focus

Present simple and present continuous

1 Read the advertisement. Do you think this is an interesting job? Say why.

2 Now complete the paragraph on the right.

Finance Manager
Granada Film

Granada Film, part of the Granada Media Group, produces and co-finances a broad range of films for the UK and international markets; films including *My Left Foot*, *Jack & Sarah*, *Girls' Night* and the soon to be released *Rogue Trader*.

Granada Media Group is an Equal Opportunities Employer and positively welcomes applications from all sections of the community.

Due to expansion we are looking for a Finance Manager with film finance experience, good communication skills and the ability to work under pressure. The successful applicant will report to the Controller of Finance and will form an integral part of a closely knit team.

Please apply in writing enclosing full CV to: **Alison Johns, Personnel Department, LWT, The London TV Centre, Upper Ground, London SE1 9LT**. Closing date 7th Aug.

Regrettably we cannot reply to all applicants, however shortlisted candidates will be contacted within 4 weeks of the closing date.

G R A N A D A   F I L M

Granada Film wants to recruit a
1 _Finance_ _Manager_.
Granada Film is part of the 2 _Granada Media Group_. The company
3 _abroad_ and 4 _cofinance_
films. _range_
They want someone with the following experience and skills:
5 _____
6 _____
7 _____
He/She will join the finance team and report to the 8 _____
_____ _____ .

To apply, send a 9 _____ and a
10 _____ to the Personnel Department.

3 Find these sentences in the advertisement and write in the verb.

1 Granada Film, part of the Granada Media Group, _____ and _____ a broad range of films for the UK and international markets.

2 Due to expansion we _____ a Finance Manager with film finance experience, good communication skills and the ability to work under pressure.

The verb in sentence 1 above is in the **present simple tense**.
The verb in sentence 2 is in the **present continuous tense**.

3 Which tense do we use to talk about a non-permanent or a current activity?

4 Which tense do we use to talk about a fact or permanent activity?

▶ **Grammar Reference page 150**

Pronunciation

Third person singular /s//z//ɪz/

1 🔊 **2.2** The 's' at the end of the *he, she, it* forms is pronounced in three different ways. Listen and notice the difference.

/s/	/z/	/ɪz/
looks	sells	produces
presents	plays	changes

2 🔊 **2.3** Now listen to these verbs. Put each group under the correct column heading /s//z/ or /ɪz/.

a welcomes	buys	applies	delivers	includes	provides	
b increases	finances	closes	publishes	watches	manages	
c stops	wants	markets	operates	takes	works	

3 Complete the rules.

> **1** For verbs that end in /p/, /t/, /k/, /f/ we pronounce the final *s* ____
>
> **2** For verbs that end in /s/, /z/, /ʃ/, /tʃ/, /dʒ/ we pronounce the final *s* ____
>
> **3** For verbs that end in all other sounds we pronounce the final *s* ____

Language Practice

1 You decide to invest some money in a company. Your final choice is between a pharmaceutical company and a cable operator.

What does each company do? Look at the pictures and use the words in the box to help you.

to develop
to manufacture
to prepare
to launch
to provide
to expand

Pharmaceutical products   *Putting down a cable*

2 🔊 **2.4** Listen to a business analyst and complete the table below.

	PHARMACEUTICAL COMPANY	CABLE OPERATOR
What the company does		
Current activities		

Reading

1 Quickly read the text below.

1 Is the text
   a a recruitment advert?
   b a news article?
   c an advert for the *Financial Times*?

2 Is the text for
   a people who have just finished university?
   b people with experience?
   c people who haven't been to university?

FINANCIAL TIMES GROUP
BUSINESS GRADUATE TRAINEE PROGRAMME

The Financial Times Group is part of Pearson plc, the international media group with interests in publishing, television production, broadcasting, and electronic and multimedia business. The Financial Times Group includes:

   The *Financial Times:* the world's best business newspaper.
   Financial Times Information: providers of electronic and specialist financial information.
   FT Business: providers of specialist business information for finance, energy, media and telecoms industries.
   FT Electronic Publishing: Europe's leading provider of electronic general business information.
   Les Echos: France's leading business daily newspaper.
   Recoletos: Spain's leading newspaper and magazine publisher.

The Financial Times Group is planning to recruit up to six business graduates for a fifteen month training programme, enabling participants to gain an overall understanding of the business. Projects may include work in strategic planning, product development, editorial, marketing and advertisement sales.

The requirements
- ability to think innovatively and practically
- a high degree of business awareness
- good communication skills
- ambition
- a wide range of interests and experience

Salary
£21,000 per annum

How to apply
Please apply, enclosing CV and covering letter, marking your envelope 'Business Graduate Trainee Programme', to the Head of Employee Relations, Financial Times, Number One Southwark Bridge, London SE 9HL

We believe in equality of opportunity and employ people solely on the basis of their abilities.

2 Read the text carefully and answer these questions.

1 What is the parent company of the Financial Times Group (FT)?

2 Which four areas does the parent company operate in?

3 Which four areas does the Financial Times Group operate in?

  a newspapers   **d** financial information   **g** business information
  b magazines   **e** television   **h** books
  c software manuals   **f** electronic information

4 Name three newspapers which the FT Group publishes.

5 What is the FT Group planning?

6 Graduate recruits can expect to gain experience in a number of areas. Name three of them.

7 What requirements does the FT have of the recruits?

8 Which of these are personal qualities? Which of these are skills or knowledge?

9 How long is the training scheme?

10 What is one of the company's beliefs?

3 Do you think this is a good company to work for?

Vocabulary   **Word building**

1 The nouns in the table are in the text. Write in the verb forms.

NOUNS	VERBS
1 production product	
2 providers provision (not in text)	
3 development	
4 marketing market (not in text)	
5 advertisement	

2 Use a verb or noun from the table to fill the gaps. (Use one noun twice.)

There are usually several different departments in a company, and they all need to work together to make the company successful. Companies offer products or services to the consumer in a competitive ¹_____. In the manufacturing sector ²_____ development is a key activity. Companies ³_____ new products and launch them on the ⁴_____. They try to keep the cost of ⁵_____ low to stay competitive. It is essential to ⁶_____ the product and to tell the consumer about it.

Listening

1 Work in pairs. Say what you know about the companies in the table.

	Virgin	UNITED COLORS OF BENETTON.	DAIMLERCHRYSLER	SONY
Nationality				
Product(s)				
Other information				

2 ⊟ 2.5 Tom Armstrong and Rachel Humphries talk about the four companies. Listen and complete the table.

Writing

Avoiding repetition

1 Each word *in italics* below refers to something already mentioned. Work in pairs and say what each word *in italics* refers to.

Does it refer to a noun? adjective? verb?

Example:

1 Many (companies) produce hamburgers. McDonald's is an internationally famous (one.)

'one' refers to a noun – 'companies'

2 Some companies are multinationals and *others* are not.

3 Reuters provides information for many different clients; *these* include newspapers and financial markets.

4 The EMI Group produces records. *The company* is also involved in music retailing.

5 DHL is an international air express carrier. *It* delivers documents and packages all over the world.

6 There are 300 HMV Group stores around the world. *They* are located in 8 countries.

7 Many fast food companies operate on a franchise basis. McDonald's is *one of them*.

2 Read the paragraph below and change the underlined words to avoid repetition.

Example:
1 *The Virgin Groups's interests include… → These include…*

> The Virgin Group has many interests. [1] <u>The Virgin Group's interests</u> include international 'Megastore' music retailing, book and software publishing, film and video editing facilities and clubs and hotels. [2] <u>The Virgin Group's interests</u> also include a model agency, Virgin Cola, and a radio station. [3] <u>The Virgin Group</u> operates many companies. Virgin Atlantic is [4] <u>a Virgin Group company</u>. Virgin Atlantic is well-known for its superior service at a competitive price.

3 Use your notes from the Listening to write a paragraph describing Virgin, Benetton, Daimler Chrysler or Sony. Try to avoid repetition.

Business Communication

Presenting information

1 ▭ 2.6 **Look at the chart of LVMH and try to answer the questions. Then listen to the presentation and check your answers.**

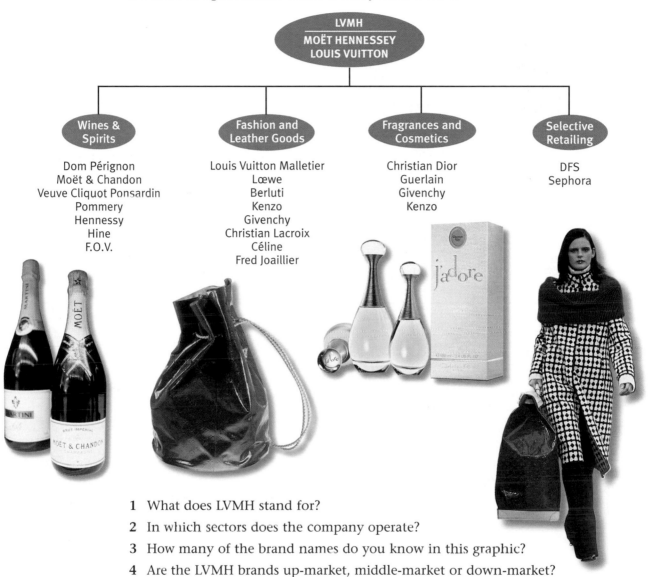

1 What does LVMH stand for?

2 In which sectors does the company operate?

3 How many of the brand names do you know in this graphic?

4 Are the LVMH brands up-market, middle-market or down-market?

Pronunciation Two

Sentence stress

2 ▭ 2.7 **Every sentence in English has stressed and unstressed parts. Listen to these sentences from the presentation and mark the stressed syllables.**

1 First of all, what does LVMH stand for?

2 Well, of course, it specialises in luxury products .... and it operates in a number of sectors.

3 Look at the brand names in each sector.

4 Each sector includes world-famous names.

5 Let's look first at wines and spirits.

Benetton skiers

3 Work in two groups, **Group 1** and **Group 2**, to find out more about Edizone Holding and Sony.

GROUP 1

Work in pairs, **Student A** and **Student B**.

Student B: Turn to page 146 to find out more about Edizione Holding.

STUDENT A

Look at the chart below which gives information about Edizione Holding. Ask Student B for information to fill in the gaps.

Ask about:

• which sectors Edizione Holding operates in
• the names of the companies

KEY

SECTORS

● = MANUFACTURING
● = FOOD RETAILING
● = REAL ESTATE AND AGRICULTURE
● = OTHER SECTORS

---

edizione holding family tree

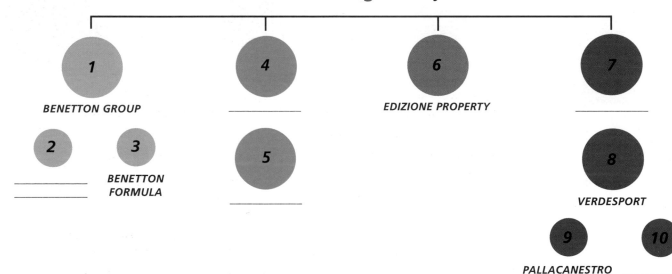

1 BENETTON GROUP

2 _____

3 BENETTON FORMULA

4 _____

5 _____

6 EDIZIONE PROPERTY

7 _____

8 VERDESPORT

9 PALLACANESTRO TREVISO

10 _____

11 OTHER MINORITY INTERESTS

GROUP 2

Work in pairs, **Student C** and **Student D**.
Student D Turn to page 146 to find out about Sony.

STUDENT C

Look at the chart on page 23 which gives information about Sony. Ask Student D for information to fill in the gaps.

Ask about:

• main areas of business
• the names of the Sony companies

SONY

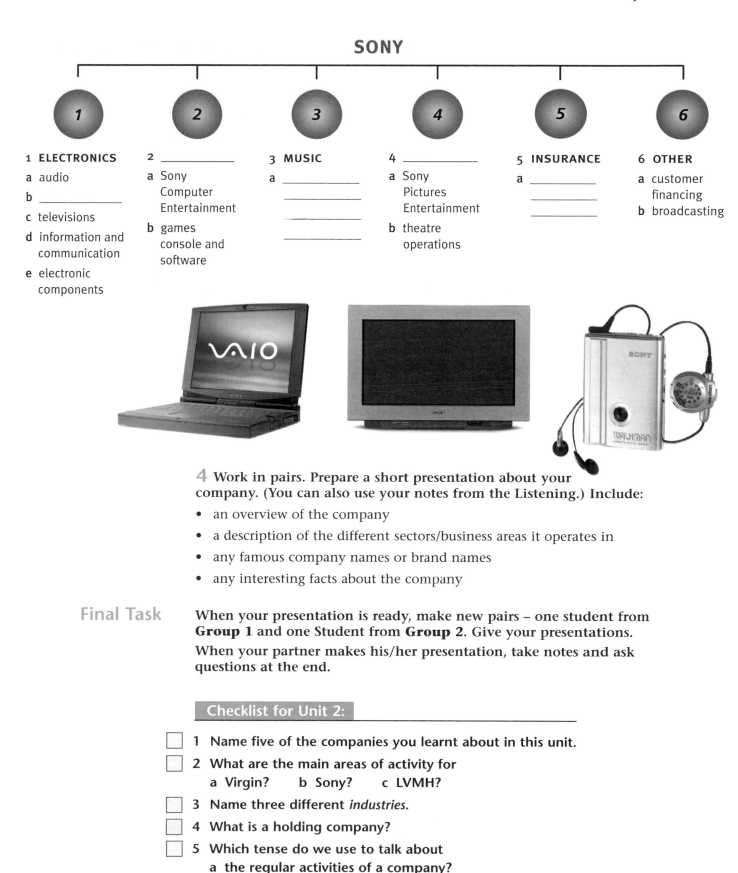

1 ELECTRONICS
a audio
b _____
c televisions
d information and communication
e electronic components

2 _____
a Sony Computer Entertainment
b games console and software

3 MUSIC
a _____
_____
_____
_____

4 _____
a Sony Pictures Entertainment
b theatre operations

5 INSURANCE
a _____
_____
_____

6 OTHER
a customer financing
b broadcasting

4 **Work in pairs. Prepare a short presentation about your company. (You can also use your notes from the Listening.) Include:**

- an overview of the company
- a description of the different sectors/business areas it operates in
- any famous company names or brand names
- any interesting facts about the company

Final Task

When your presentation is ready, make new pairs – one student from Group 1 and one Student from Group 2. Give your presentations.

When your partner makes his/her presentation, take notes and ask questions at the end.

Checklist for Unit 2:

☐ 1 Name five of the companies you learnt about in this unit.

☐ 2 What are the main areas of activity for
   a Virgin?   b Sony?   c LVMH?

☐ 3 Name three different *industries*.

☐ 4 What is a holding company?

☐ 5 Which tense do we use to talk about
   a the regular activities of a company?
   b the current activities of a company?

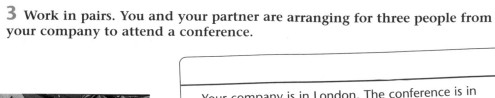

3 Work in pairs. You and your partner are arranging for three people from your company to attend a conference.

> Your company is in London. The conference is in Paris. The conference is for one day, starting at 10.00 a.m. and finishing at 5.30 p.m. There is a dinner the evening before.
>
> Decide which method of transport would be best for Dr Brook, Ms Turner and Mr Brown.
>
> Think about these things:
> - journey times
> - how easy your plan is for each person
> - price

Information

	PRICE	TIME	FIRST/LAST	OTHER
EUROSTAR London – Paris	£229	3hrs	0515/2113	
BA Heathrow – Paris CDG	£270.50 + tax	1 hr 10 mins	0720/2015	
STENA SEALINK Dover – Calais	£25 per car	75-90 mins	25 sailings daily. Depart every 45 mins	extra passengers = £1 each
HOVERSPEED HOVERCRAFT Dover – Calais SEA CAT	£78 £78	35 mins 55 mins	0700/2030 0700/2330	
LE SHUTTLE Folkestone – Calais	£190 with car	35 mins	24 hour service	day return = £95 valid for 5 days

1 **Dr Brook** is travelling from central London to give a conference paper. He wants to attend the dinner.

2 **Ms Turner** is travelling from central London to attend the conference. She has a meeting after the conference with the Sales Director from 6.00 – 8.00 p.m. She doesn't want to travel by Eurostar.

3 **Mr Brown** is travelling from Dover. He is going by car as he is visiting his son who lives in Paris. He wants to stay a few days, but he isn't sure of his return date.

Compare your decision with a different partner. Explain your choice.

Vocabulary One

Word partners (making arrangements)

1 Match a word on the left with a word on the right to make a common word partnership.

1	to run	**a**	a conference
2	to hold	**b**	a meal
3	to plan	**c**	a party
4	to book	**d**	a subsidiary
5	to throw	**e**	a ticket
6	to visit	**f**	an itinerary
7	to order	**g**	a seminar

2 Work in pairs. Make sentences using each word partner then make an offer or a request.

Example:
I'm running a seminar next month. Would you like to be a speaker?

Writing

Faxes

You are going on a business trip to Australia. Send a fax to your Australian colleague, Sally Jones, to tell her about the arrangements. Ask her to make hotel bookings and hire a car for you. Use the notes below.

Trip to Melbourne – November 7th 2001

Arrangements:
· flight – BA 135T Heathrow, London 1300; arrive Melbourne 0800 November 8th
· Hotel Ramada Inn – November 8th – 11th
· Visit regional offices – November 9th
· Visit Head Office in Victoria – November 12th
· flight BA 136F Victoria – November 13th

To book:
· transport from airport – Ramada Inn
· hire car to go to regional offices – November 9th
· hotel for night of November 12th – Victoria

MetaCom

Manor Park Parade
London
SE13 1XS

FAX MESSAGE

To: Sally Jones
Fax No: 0011 61 39452

From:
Fax No: +44 (0)171 123 4567
Date:
Re:

Pages (including this one): 1

Message

This is to let you know about the arrangements for my trip to Australia next week. I'm taking flight BA135T . . . .

Could you . . . .
. . . .

► **Business Writing
page 68 Workbook**

Listening

International travel

1 📼 **3.5 Listen to Colin Knapp talking about travelling to the Far East.**

1 How often does Colin travel on business?

2 Which country does he visit regularly?

3 How long is the flight?

4 What two things does he do during the flight?

5 Does he suffer from jet lag?

6 Is jet lag different travelling west–east and east–west?

7 Why does he travel to the Far East instead of doing business by telephone or fax?

8 What example of a culture gap does he give?

9 What three tips does he give for visiting this country for the first time?

2 Work in groups and discuss these questions.

• Do you like or dislike flying?

• Do you sleep on a plane or do you prefer to read? Do you always watch the in-flight film?

• What do you know about jet lag?

• Have you experienced cultural differences when you travel?

• What are the advantages of face-to-face meetings compared to doing business by telephone, fax or computer?

Reading

1 The article is about Japanese people in Britain. Before you read, work in pairs and discuss these questions.

1 Would you like to live or work in a foreign country? Why/Why not?

2 What do you think are the cultural differences between the Japanese and the British?

2 Read paragraphs 1–4 of the article and answer the questions.

1 How many Japanese work in Britain?

2 What is Masami Sato's job title?

3 Does Masami Sato like living and working in London? Why/Why not?

4 Why is she working in London?

5 What are her job opportunities in London?

6 When is she going home?

7 Does she want to go home? Why/Why not?

3 Now read paragraphs 5 and 6 of the article and answer the questions.

1 In what way is life in Britain difficult for Japanese?

2 Describe one cultural difference between Japanese and British people.

Made in Japan, Sold on Britain

54,400 Japanese live in Britain. How do they find life here?

1 54,400 Japanese live in Britain: 12,000 are business people, 5,800 are students, most of the rest are their families. The Japanese like Britain. They find it strange, but they like it.

2 Masami Sato, one of only 70 'office ladies' – junior women managers – in Britain, is happy. She says, 'most things are better here than in Tokyo – there are so many parks and green fields'.

3 As an office lady, she cannot be promoted above her present junior managerial position, but she thinks the UK is less male-dominated than Japan. She is in London as part of a scheme to give office ladies overseas experience (they are allowed to go to 10 cities considered safe – none of them are in the United States), and she does not want to go back to Tokyo when the time comes next year.

4 'When I go back to Japan, I have to live with my family,' she says. 'There are few amusements and we can't be relaxed because all Japanese are very busy.'

5 The Japanese appreciate the space, the more relaxed atmosphere and the longer holidays, but they also experience some difficulties: the most obvious is the language. Mr Kojima has lived in Wales for two years, and still has problems. 'The language is very difficult, but the staff are very experienced at explaining to the Japanese,' he says. 'I can understand the explanations, but I can't understand when they talk to each other.'

6 Besides the language, there are also cultural differences which can make life difficult. Banker Kaoru Itoh says 'the British like arguments, the Japanese don't. They dislike raising the opposite opinion. In Japan everyone respects the opinion of the majority.' ●

The Independent on Sunday

4 **Work in pairs and discuss.**

Do you think it is easy or difficult for Japanese to meet British people socially? Why/Why not?

Vocabulary Two

Adjectives of nationality

1 Adjectives of nationality have five different types of ending.

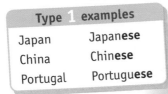

Type 1 examples

Japan	Japan**ese**
China	Chin**ese**
Portugal	Portugu**ese**

Type 4 examples

Sweden	Swed**ish**
Spain	Span**ish**
Turkey	Turk**ish**

Type 2 examples

America	Americ**an**
Germany	Germ**an**
South Africa	South Afric**an**
Europe	Europ**ean**

Type 5 examples

Saudi Arabia	Saud**i**
Kuwait	Kuwait**i**
Pakistan	Pakistan**i**

Type 3 examples

Australia	Austral**ian**
Russia	Russ**ian**
Nigeria	Niger**ian**
Asia	As**ian**

Work in pairs. What are the adjectives of nationality for these countries?
They all have an ending from the list above.

a Belgium   e Denmark   i Ireland   m Mexico

b Brazil   f Finland   j Oman   n Poland

c Britain   g Hungary   k Italy   o Singapore

d Canada   h Bahrain   l Malta   p Vietnam

2 The adjectives of nationality for the following countries do not use the five endings above. Do you know what they are?

1 France _____

2 Greece _____

3 The Netherlands _____

4 Switzerland _____

5 Thailand _____

What is the adjective of nationality for your country?

Cross-cultural Comparison

Test your cross-cultural knowledge with this quiz.

Quiz
Do you have good cross-cultural skills?

When you meet someone for the first time, what should you do?

True(T) or False(F)?

a It's usual to shake hands the first time you meet a British colleague. (T)

b It's not a good idea to call German colleagues by their first names at work. ◯

c When a Japanese business person gives you his/her business card, it's polite to say thank you and put it in your pocket. ◯

d In the Mediterranean, embrace colleagues when you meet them. ◯

e Take off your shoes when you visit someone's house in Poland. ◯

f In Saudi Arabia it is rude to refuse a cup of coffee. ◯

g In the UK, ask about your host's family when you meet for the first time. ◯

h In Asian countries, it is rude to look people in the eyes. ◯

i British people like to talk about their salaries. ◯

j When you visit Poland, your host gives you flowers at the airport. ◯

Now check your answers on page 147

Business Communication

Introductions and socialising

1 📼 3.6 Listen to six introductions and match the names.

1	Miss Kim	**a**	Duncan Grove
2	Barry	**b**	Fiona
3	Caroline Courtney	**c**	Sofia
4	Stephen Brown	**d**	David Walker
5	Señor Iglesias	**e**	Ms Barty
6	John Smith	**f**	Mr Kinzett

2 📼 3.6 Listen again. Write one more example in each box below.

Introducing someone	**Responding to an introduction**	**Introducing yourself**
• I'd like to introduce you to Señor Iglesias.	• How do you do?	• How do you do?
• Mr Brown, this is Ms Barty.	• Pleased to meet you.	• I'm John Smith.

3 Work in pairs. Introduce yourselves then introduce a third person.

Customers, Companies and Travel

Business Review

Work in pairs. Choose three of the following companies.

Marks & Spencer	Kwik-Fit	LVMH
Sony	McDonald's	First Direct bank

1 What does each company do? What are its products or services?

2 What nationality is each company?

3 What does each company try to give its customers? What is it committed to?

Vocabulary Review

1 All the words below are key words from units 1, 2 and 3. Work in pairs and put each word into the correct list.

1 repeat business	10	itinerary
2 parent company	11	colleagues
3 buying	12	subsidiaries
4 code of practice	13	sector
5 customer loyalty	14	selling
6 cultural difference	15	marketing
7 foreign business trip	16	multinational
8 jet lag	17	production
9 customer care	18	social conventions

Customers	Companies	Travel

2 Give a definition for each word.

3 How many other key words from units 1, 2 or 3 can you add to the lists?

Grammar Review

Direct and indirect questions

1 You are at a conference and decide to attend a presentation to find out more about the FT Group's training programmes.

1 Write five questions that you want to ask the speaker about:

a work experience for trainees

b opportunities to specialise

c work on well-known newspapers

d possibility of working for the company after training course

NOTE: Remember: indirect questions are formal/polite.

2 Work in pairs. Ask and answer the questions. Student A is the speaker, Student B asks the questions first. Then change roles.

2 Work in groups of three.

Students A and B: You are graduates on the FT training programme.
Student C: Introduce yourself and find out about Students A and B and about the programme.

Prepare your roles first!

Present simple and present continuous

3 Read the text and choose the correct tense for the verbs in brackets. ( )

British Airways is an international airline which (carry) [1]_____ over 28 million passengers each year. They (look) [2]_____ for graduates with potential for management.
SmithKline Beecham is a transnational healthcare company. SB (be) [3]_____ involved in research, development, production and marketing of healthcare products, and (employ) [4]_____ 54,000 people worldwide.
Aldi is a large, international food retailer. It (have) [5]_____ over 100 stores in the UK, and (open) [6]_____ many new stores.

Present continuous for future

4 Fill in the diary pages with things that you are doing this week.

Monday

Tuesday

Wednesday

Thursday

Friday

Saturday/Sunday

Now work in pairs. Try to arrange a meeting at a time when you are both free. Use the language in the box to help you.

What are you doing on ......?
I can't meet you on ...... I'm ......
Yes, that's fine. I'm not doing anything then.

Writing and Business Communication Review

1 Read the information about Boeing and answer the questions. Ignore punctuation for the moment.

1 What does Boeing do?

2 What three sectors does Boeing operate in?

3 Where is the company based? What nationality is the company?

the Boeing company is an enormous American aerospace company which manufactures aircraft. over 400 airlines use boeing aircraft. boeing manufactures civil aircraft. boeing manufactures military aeroplanes and boeing develops advanced computer technology. the us government buys its military planes, systems and space vehicles from boeing.

boeing's headquarters are in Seattle, Washington State. 87,000 people work for boeing in Seattle. over 116,000 work directly for boeing in the USA and Canada. 60% of boeing's sales are overseas.

2 Re-write the paragraphs. This time make sure:

• that capital letters are used properly

• that you avoid repetition. Think about which nouns are repeated and which words can replace them. *(the company, it, they, these, one, one of them, others)*

3 Use the paragraphs to prepare a short company presentation. Include:

• what the company specialises in / what sectors it operates in

• famous brand names

• main customer(s)

• where the company is based

4 *Troubleshooting*

Key Vocabulary

Sometimes companies realise that they are not achieving their **goals** or objectives effectively, that is, they are not getting the results they need. In this case they have to re-plan their **strategy**. It can be useful to get an outsider, e.g. a **management consultant**, to analyse the company's performance and recommend changes to make it more efficient. A **SWOT analysis** can be useful, that is, an analysis of the company's strengths (S) and weaknesses (W) and also of the opportunities (O) and threats (T) that face the company. **Troubleshooting,** or solving problems, is a necessary part of running a company.

Lead-in

1 The fashion model agency IMG solves a problem through successful troubleshooting strategies. Read the text and complete the notes.

A Model Manager

Company	IMG
History	One of the best-known model agencies in the industry for many years with an excellent reputation as a fashionable, forward-looking company.
The problem	The company loses its reputation as one of the best and needs a new strategy.
The solution	The board appoints a new Managing Director, Jonathan Phang. He has over fifteen years of experience in the model industry.
The strategy	Jonathan's main tasks are to find new models; to generate more awareness of what the agency is all about, and to encourage girls from other agencies to switch* to IMG. He also has to cut costs to make the agency more profitable and stop representing models who aren't making money.
The result	IMG is now attracting excellent models which means they are also attracting more clients and doing well financially.

* *to switch:* to change

Past problem:	The company's [1]_____ was in danger.
Solution:	Recruit [2]_____.
The strategy:	• Make the agency well-known.
	• Persuade [3]_____ to join the agency.
	• Reduce [4]_____ and improve [5]_____.
	• Not represent models [6]_____.
The results:	• [7]_____ join the company.
	• The company has more [8]_____.
	• The company makes more [9]_____.

2 Work in pairs and use the points below to complete a SWOT analysis for IMG at the time Jonathan Phang joined the company.

• In the past – one of the best known companies.

• Model agency business is very competitive. A lot of other agencies are looking for good models too.

• IMG no longer has a reputation for being fashionable or forward-looking.

• New MD has a lot of experience.

• IMG is looking for new models.

• IMG has models who are not earning money for the company.

• MD has ability to make good financial decisions.

• All model agencies are looking for new models.

• Models switch to good agencies quickly.

• Profits can be excellent for a successful company.

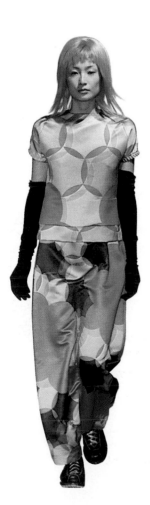

STRENGTHS

New MD has a lot of experience

WEAKNESSES

OPPORTUNITIES

THREATS

3 Compare your SWOT analysis with a new partner. Are there any differences? If there are, why?

Language Focus

Should and *ought to*: making recommendations

1 ▭ 4.2 **Two women talk about the way companies sell cars. Listen and put the five things they discuss in the order you hear them.**

a women selling cars ☐

b children's car seats and car phones ☐

c 'soft sell' from dealers ☐

d car dealers and manufacturers taking women more seriously ☐

e adverts containing product information ☐

2 ▭ **Listen again and complete the recommendations for change.**

1 Car Dealers

a Yes, they _____ _____ us seriously.

b Yes, they _____ _____ more women selling cars.

c The dealers are always men. I think they _____ _____ _____ a soft-sell approach.

2 Special Features

Children's car seats and car phones _____ _____ available as standard.

3 Adverts

a They _____ _____ the adverts, too.

b Yes, I think there _____ _____ lots of product information in adverts.

c They _____ _____ _____ us about things like petrol consumption.

3 **Which two verbs do the women use to recommend change?**

1 **Are these verbs followed by**

   a infinitive?   b infinitive without *to*?   c gerund?

2 **How do you make these sentences negative?**

   a *They should listen to women.*

   b *They ought to include car phones in all new cars.*

3 **How do you ask a question with *should/ought to*?**

Now check your answers with the Grammar reference.

▶ **Grammar Reference page 153**

Pronunciation

Polite intonation

1 ▭ 4.3 When you make a recommendation using *should*, make sure your voice falls at the end of the sentence. Listen to these sentences.

1 They should take women more seriously.

2 They should fit car phones.

3 The adverts should give more information.

2 ▭ 4.4 Now listen and repeat.

Language Practice

1 Match each situation with a suitable recommendation or solution.

SITUATION	SOLUTION
1 We are losing our reputation as a first-class agency.	a We should try to offer something special and focus on excellent customer care.
2 Many of our models are not making money for the agency.	b The shareholders are very unhappy about this. We should find ways to improve the situation quickly.
3 The costs of running the agency are very high.	c The MD should decide not to represent these girls. He ought to attract new models.
4 The financial position is very weak.	d We should think of ways of reducing them.
5 The model agency business is very competitive.	e We should appoint someone with a new strategy to run the company.

2 Here is some advice on how to deal effectively with problems.

Which advice do you follow? Tick (✓) the boxes.

☐ ❶ Don't avoid a problem, deal with it.

☐ ❷ Don't see all problems as other people's problems. Focus on yourself.

☐ ❸ Don't blame people, look for solutions.

☐ ❹ Look at a problem as an opportunity – to learn something or to achieve something.

☐ ❺ Think ahead to prevent problems.

☐ ❻ When something is important, deal with it. Don't wait until it becomes urgent.

☐ ❼ Don't always look for 'quick fixes', or temporary solutions. Identify the real cause of the problem and work to find a solution to this.

☐ ❽ Don't try to change the things you can't change. Learn to accept them.

3 Now work with a partner. How are you similar and how are you different? Give each other advice.

Reading

1 The text is about Ford, the car manufacturer. In the Language Focus, Belinda and Anna made the following points:

a An increasing number of women buy cars nowadays.

b Car manufacturers should aim their advertisements at male and female buyers.

c Car manufacturers and car dealers should take women buyers seriously and think about the different needs of male and female buyers.

Read the first paragraph only and say which of these points the writer makes.

2 Read the text and complete the summary on page 41.

Car giant sends in the spy girls

Hit squad to check on deals for women

by DAVID BENSON Motoring Editor

1 FORD has set up a female 'spy' team to visit dealers and make sure they treat women car buyers seriously and with respect.

2 The company says women now buy four out of every 10 new cars sold in Britain.

3 This is the highest proportion in Europe where the women buyers' share averages three in ten.

4 And Ford says the proportion of women buyers will continue to increase in the next decade.

5 The company's International Women's Marketing Panel will ensure that its products and service meet the needs of female customers and that they get a fair deal.

6 It claims to be the only European car maker to have such a panel.

7 The team is made up of British women Ford workers and others from nine European countries. It has 16 permanent members supported by a sub-committee of 40. "It's views are keenly sought* in research and vehicle appraisal programmes.*" said a Ford spokesman.

8 "The panel's members also participate in advertising clinics* and go on 'mystery shops' during which they visit dealerships posing as* prospective buyers."

9 "Reports are then fed back to senior management so that recommendations can be considered in future plans."

* *keenly sought:* [the panel's opinions] are taken very seriously
* *appraisal programmes:* a series of tests
* *advertising clinic:* a place to brainstorm or discuss ideas about advertising
* *to pose as:* to pretend or make believe

The Express

Ford Motor Company has a [1.]_____' team called the International [2]_____. The team has [3]_____ members and is made up of British [4]_____ and others from [5]_____ European countries. Their purpose is to visit dealers to check that [6]_____ take women's views and experiences seriously because women buy [7]_____ out of every [8]_____ cars in Britain. The team write [9]_____ for [10]_____ so that they can make recommendations for the future.

3 Work in pairs and do a SWOT analysis for Ford.

Vocabulary

Synonyms

1 Look at these phrases from the article on Ford. All three refer to the same thing, in other words they are *synonyms*.

car giant	Ford	car maker

Match a phrase on the left with a synonym phrase on the right.

PHRASE	SYNONYM
1 women's marketing panel	a to visit dealerships
2 women car buyers	b to ensure
3 to tour dealers	c female 'spy' team
4 to make sure	d female customers

Word building

2 Complete the table with words from the text.

NOUN	VERB
1	to buy
2 an increase	
3	to produce
4 participation	
5 a visit	
6	to recommend

3 Choose five words from exercise 2 and write a sentence using each.

4 Answer these questions about the past simple tense.

1 How is the regular past simple tense formed?
e.g. start**ed**, back**ed**, open**ed**

2 Not all verbs have a regular past simple tense. Give an example of an irregular past simple tense from the text on page 47.

3 Look at the two questions (a and b). Underline the *auxiliary verb* ⁓⁓⁓ and the *main verb* _ _ _ _ _ _ for each.
a When *did it all start?'*
b When *did it come to Britain?*

4 Look at the two negative sentences and underline the *negative auxiliary verb* ⁓⁓⁓ and the *main verb* _ _ _ _ _ _ for each:
a *Ford built the first car in 1896, but he did not form the company until 1903.*
b *The first truck didn't roll off the line until 1931.*

Now look at the grammar reference to check your answers.

▶ **Grammar Reference page 152**

Pronunciation

Past simple verb endings

1 There are three different pronunciations for the regular past simple tense ending *-ed*. They are /t/, /d/ and /ɪd/.

> 🔲 **5.3 Listen and repeat.**
>
> 1 We use /t/ after the sounds /p/, /tʃ/, /k/, /f/, /s/ and /ʃ/:
> *stopped, watched, worked, puffed, missed, finished.*
>
> 2 We use /ɪd/ after verbs ending in /d/ and /t/:
> *started, waited, ended.*
>
> 3 We use /d/ after all other sounds:
> *formed, rolled, opened.*

2 🔲 **5.4 Listen to the sentences and repeat them.**

1 He formed a company.

2 They started making cars.

3 They stopped making Model B trucks.

3 Practise saying the verbs in Language Focus exercise 3 on page 47.

Language Practice

1 Read this history of Dr. Martens shoes. The writer uses the present tense to make the summary seem 'alive'.

Dr. AirWair Martens WITH Bouncing SOLES

1946 A German doctor Klaus Maertens, living in Seeshaupt, near Munich, <u>goes</u> skiing and injures his foot.

He <u>makes</u> himself a pair of shoes from old tyres with air soles to cushion the foot.

Dr Maertens and a friend, Dr Herbert Funck, an engineer, <u>patent</u>* and <u>develop</u> the Doctor Maertens shoe.

1959 Maertens and Funck <u>sell</u> the manufacturing rights to R. Griggs and Co., a traditional British bootmaker.

1 April 1960 The first British DMs <u>go</u> on sale.

Mid 1960s British youth <u>adopt</u> the DM as a symbol of their anti-establishment* attitudes.

1970s Unemployed youth <u>wear</u> DMs and behave violently on football terraces. The Police wear DMs to catch them.

1971 Rebels* wear DMs in Stanley Kubrick's violent film *A Clockwork Orange*.

1975 Elton John wears giant DMs in the rock-opera *Tommy*.

Mid 1970s Punk rock fans adopt them.

1980s Thousands of Japanese, American and European youth <u>come</u> to London's Camden market to buy DMs.

1983 Young designer Wayne Heminway and his wife-to-be Geraldine, <u>set up</u> a stall in Camden market selling clothes and DMs. It <u>becomes</u> *the* place to buy DMs.

Griggs supplies Heminway with customised* DMs for his Red or Dead fashion shows.

Some women wear them as a form of protest.

1985 Madonna wears DMs in the film *Desperately Seeking Susan*.

1992 Designers such as Karl Lagerfeld and Gianni Versace <u>offer</u> designer DMs.

1993 The Pope wears them walking in the Alps and we hear the Dalai Lama <u>likes</u> them too.

Today the Vatican Guard wear them.

* *patent*: to get a legal document to stop others manufacturing a product
* *anti-establishment*: not in agreement with government or authority
* *rebel*: someone who fights against authority
* *customised*: designed for a particular customer

Klaus Maertens

Source: *The European*

2 Write the past simple forms of the verbs underlined above.

Elton John

3 Which of the past simple verbs are regular and which are irregular?

4 Look at the text again and write four questions for your partner.

Example:
When did Klaus Maertens injure his foot? Was it in a) 1896 b) 1920 c) 1946?

Now answer your partner's questions.

5 Faith Walker talks about her first pair of Dr. Martens (DMs). Before you listen, work with a partner and complete the questions the interviewer asks.

1 When did you _____ ? **4** What colour _____ ?

2 How much _____ ? **5** Why _____ ?

3 Where _____ ? **6** Do you still _____ ?

6 ▭ 5.5 Listen and see if you were right, then note the answer to each question.

Reading **1** The text is about the French company, Bic. Can you name three of Bic's products? Now quickly read the text to check.

2 What are the advantages of disposable or 'throwaway' products?

Bic's success in a throwaway world

1   FEW companies can say that they are responsible for changing the everyday habits of billions of people throughout the world, but the French company Bic, founded in 1950, is one that can.

2   The ballpoint pen came first. The original biros – named after Lazlo Biro, their Hungarian inventor – were expensive and difficult to use. Baron Marcel Bich, the owner of a small office supplies company, brought together French and British scientists to refine* and modify* the design. He negotiated the rights to produce and sell the pen with Biro. Production of the Bic "Crystal" began in 1953. The "Crystal" had a clear blue plastic tube and a visible ink supply which was sufficient to draw a

Bic is a household name, synonymous with a disposable age*

· ·

line three kilometres long.

3   Sales rose from around 50,000 a week in the first year to a quarter of a million a day by 1956. Today sales of Bic writing instruments total more than 20 million a day in 160 countries.

4   Bich was not content with a one-product business and wanted to find other throwaway ideas. In 1972 came the disposable lighter. It is another success story which made Bic world leaders in the sector, with daily sales of disposable lighters now numbering almost 4 million.

Bic's winning formula was a combination of simplicity of production and reliability; the company claims that its lighters will work 3,000 times compared with competing brands' 1,000.

5   The company used healthy profits to invest in its third major product range – the throwaway razor – in 1975. It now contests market leadership with Gillette.* Bic subsequently diversified further – into windsurfing boards and fashion – but the three original throwaway ideas remain its success stories.

* *synonymous with a disposable age:* [Bic] represents our fast-moving world
* *to refine:* improve
* *to modify:* make small changes
* *Gillette:* major manufacturer of razors and toiletries.

The European

3 Read the text and complete this company history.

COMPANY HISTORY

1950	The company was founded.
1950–53	Lazlo Biro invented the first pen.
	Marcel Bich ^{1}_____ and ^{2}_____ the design.
	Bich negotiated with Biro to ^{3}_____.
1953	Production of the ^{4}_____ began.
1956	Sales of the biro rose to ^{5}_____.
1972	Bic invented ^{6}_____.
1975	Bic invented ^{7}_____.
Now	Bic sells ^{8}_____ ballpoint pens per day.
	Bic sells ^{9}_____ disposable lighters per day.
	Bic and ^{10}_____ are leaders in the market for disposable razors.

Vocabulary

Word partners: adjectives and nouns

1 Match the adjectives with the nouns to make six word partners.

ADJECTIVE	NOUN
1 product	**a** age (heading)
2 disposable	**b** name (heading)
3 household	**c** habits (para 1)
4 healthy	**d** brand (para 4)
5 competing	**e** profits (para 5)
6 everyday	**f** range (para 5)

2 Now combine the adjectives with these nouns.

a object	**b** lighter	**c** companies	**d** competition	**e** development

Cross-cultural Comparison

Work in pairs and discuss.

1 Are disposable products popular in your country?

2 What disposable products do you use and why?

3 Are disposable products good for the environment?

Writing

Sequencing ideas

1 Number the items in the order that Bic produced them.

a razor ☐   b biro ☐   c lighter ☐   d windsurfing board ☐

2 The following sequencers describe the order of events. Read the paragraph below about Bic's history and say how they are used.

first	first of all	firstly	
second	secondly		
then	after that	afterwards	next
lastly	finally	now/today	

Bic is well-known for its disposable products. **First of all**, Bic produced the throwaway pen, the biro. **Then** came the disposable lighter. **Next** they invented the throwaway razor and **after that** the windsurfing board. **Today** the company focuses on producing razors, biros and lighters. There were three key inventions in the company's history: **firstly** the ballpoint pen, **secondly** the disposable lighter and **lastly** the throwaway razor.

3 Work in pairs to find out about EMI (Electrical Musical Industries), one of the world's leading music companies.

Student B: Turn to page 147.
Student A: Study this information on EMI.
Ask and answer questions to find out the history of EMI's products.

Example:
When did EMI introduce long playing vinyl records?
What did it do in 1952?

Date	Event
_____	EMI introduced long playing vinyl records (LPs).
1952	_____
_____	EMI introduced stereo LP recordings (LPs).
1966	_____
1983	EMI launched its first compact discs.
1994	_____
Today	One of the world's leading music companies.

4 Write a history of EMI's music production. Use the description of Bic in exercise 2 to help you.

 Grammar Reference page 158

Listening

Zurich Financial District

1 Pat Woodgate describes the history of the company he works for, Zurich Financial Services Group. Before you listen, match the words on the left with a definition on the right.

1	asset management	**a**	a sum of money is paid to a company to take on a risk for you
2	insurance	**b**	a company gives you financial advice, then manages your possessions
3	re-insurance	**c**	to join together to form a new company
4	to merge	**d**	an insurance company buys its own insurance from other insurance companies, to share the risk of loss

2 🔲 5.6a **Listen to the first part of the talk and answer the questions.**

1 Which two things does the presenter talk about?

2 Complete the sentences.

    a Pat works in the Loss Control Department of Zurich _____, part of the Zurich _____ _____ Group.

    b The company deals with the *p*_____ *s*_____, e.g. local _____ and National Health trusts.

3 Where was the company founded?

4 In English, what was its original name?

3 🔲 5.6b **Here are the key dates in the company's history. Listen to the second part of the talk and match each event to the correct date.**

    a 1873   **b** 1875   **c** 1922   **d** 1993   **e** 1998

1 The company merged with British American Financial Services and formed Zurich Financial Services Group. _____

2 The company obtained a licence to conduct business in other European countries. _____

3 The company opened for business in the UK, with headquarters in London. _____

4 The company started business and provided re-insurance. _____

5 The company took over the business of Municipal Mutual Insurance (MMI). _____

4 Complete the missing information.

Employees:	The group has [1]_____ employees.
Customers:	The group has over [2]_____ customers.
Countries:	The group operates in [3]_____ countries.
Company status:	One of the ten largest companies which offer [4]_____.

Business Communication

Company presentation

1 Work in two groups and prepare a presentation.

GROUP A

You represent Bic, and are preparing a presentation on the history of the company to give to a group of university graduates. Use the notes from the Reading (page 50) and the information below to prepare your presentation.

GROUP B

You represent EMI and are preparing a presentation on the history of the company to give to a group of university graduates. Use the notes from the Writing (page 52) and the information below to prepare your presentation.

Introduction

In the introduction you should tell your audience what you are going to say. Use the sequencing words you practised in the Writing section to explain the sequence.

> '**Firstly** I'm going to talk to you today about the key developments in the history of the company I work for and **then** tell you about the company's current position.'

Main Body of the Presentation

Now prepare the body of the presentation. Don't write the presentation, but make notes to help you remember what you want to say. Use the language in the box to tell the listener about the sequence of events.

> There are (six) key dates in the company's history …
>
> Firstly, in 1950 …
>
> After that …
>
> Is that clear?
>
> Lastly …
>
> Now the company is a leader in the field of …
>
> Are there any questions?
>
> Thank you very much.

2 Work in pairs, one from Group A and one from Group B.

Student A: Give your presentation to your partner who is a graduate at a local university. Be enthusiastic about your company – you want to impress your partner!

Student B: Ask Student A questions at the end of the presentation. Discuss the strengths and weaknesses of the presentation. Ask yourself these questions:

- How **clear** was the message?   Was it easy to follow?
- How **fluent** was your partner?   Did he/she speak without many hesitations?
- How **accurate** was your partner?   Did he/she make many mistakes?
- How **confident** was your partner?

Now change roles. Student B: Give your presentation to Student A.
Student A: Listen, ask questions and comment on the presentation.

Final Task   Choose one of the companies you have studied so far.

Write a short summary of the history of the company. Be careful with past tense verbs and remember to use sequencing words to help your reader.

Checklist for Unit 5:

☐ 1   What do you know about Ford?

☐ 2   What is the past tense of: *make, develop, build, sell, go?*

☐ 3   Name three Bic products.

☐ 4   How do you pronounce these regular past tense verbs?
      a *stopped*   b *worked*   c *opened*   d *formed*   e *started*   f *ended*

☐ 5   Describe two key events in the company history of Zurich Financial Services Group.

6 *Retailing*

Key Vocabulary

6.1 Retailing is the provision of **goods** or **services** to the customer. **Retailers** buy goods directly from the **manufacturer** or from a **wholesaler**, (the 'middleman'), and make their income from the **margin**, or difference, between the price they pay for the goods and the price they sell the goods at to the **consumer**. A **retail outlet** is the place where customers can purchase goods, for example, a **supermarket** or a **department store**. Nowadays, many customers are shopping from home: shopping by **the Internet**, **TV shopping channels** or **mail-order catalogues** is becoming very popular.

Lead-in

1 Work in pairs. Look at the bar chart which shows reasons why people don't like shopping. Discuss these questions.

1 What are the two main reasons people don't like shopping?

2 What can retailers do about these two problems in your opinion?

2 Do you like shopping?

3 What do you think about catalogue shopping, Internet shopping and 24 hour shopping?

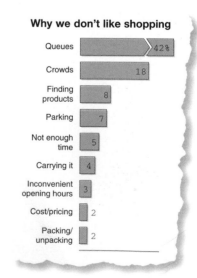

Why we don't like shopping

Queues	42%
Crowds	18
Finding products	8
Parking	7
Not enough time	5
Carrying it	4
Inconvenient opening hours	3
Cost/pricing	2
Packing/ unpacking	2

Vocabulary One

Two branches of a chain store

Word groups: Retail Sales

1 The consumer often buys a product or service from a retail outlet.
Match the types of retail outlet with the correct definition.

RETAIL OUTLET	DEFINITION
1 supermarket	**a** a very large supermarket often located on the edge of a town or city
2 hypermarket	**b** one of a group of shops owned by the same company
3 shopping centre/mall	**c** a large shop with many departments or sections – each department sells a different type of goods
4 department store	**d** a large self-service shop selling food and drink and also small household items
5 specialist retailer	**e** a covered area with shops, supermarkets and restaurants
6 chain store	**f** a shop which only sells one type of product, usually of high quality

2 Work in groups and discuss retailing in your country.

1 Do the types of retail outlet above exist in your country?
Can you name a well-known shop/outlet in each category?

2 Which shops are popular with local people and which are more popular with tourists?

3 Which shops have a reputation for quality? for reasonable prices? for exclusive or upmarket products?

3 Now ask which retail outlets students in your group buy the following goods from:

food	drink	jewellery	stereo equipment	computers	clothes

Direct Sales

4 Other methods of selling are *direct* and do not use retail outlets.
Match a definition to each example of direct sales.

Mail order catalogues

DIRECT SALES	DEFINITION
1 mail order	**a** customers can buy from the manufacturer's warehouse
2 door-to-door sales	**b** a company sends goods by post from its warehouse
3 TV sales	**c** customers see product adverts on the screen and place their orders by phone/fax/the Internet
4 The Internet (e-commerce)	**d** an agent for the company sells the product or service to the customer at home
5 cash and carry	**e** electronic shopping from companies' websites

Cross-cultural Comparison

British people now spend £6.52 billion per year buying goods through mail-order catalogues, direct selling, TV shopping channels and the Internet. **Work in pairs and discuss these questions.**

1 Do people in your country shop from home?

2 What effect does home shopping have on shops?

3 Do many people use the Internet to shop in your country? Why/Why not?

Countable and uncountable nouns

Language Focus One

1 Which of these nouns are countable and which are uncountable?

> **1** consumer(s)   **2** product(s)   **3** computer(s)   **4** information
> **5** entertainment   **6** protection   **7** shopping   **8** advice   **9** shop(s)

Articles *an, the* and zero article *(Ø)*

2 Notice the nouns **in bold** in these sentences.

COUNTABLE

a He works in **a shop** *(singular)*. **The shop** *(singular noun already referred to)* is called Xanadu.

b Many of **the shops** *(plural noun, specific)* on Fifth Avenue in New York are department stores.

Shops *(plural, general)* like this one are becoming out of date.

UNCOUNTABLE

c You can find **information** *(singular, general)* about this on the Internet.

d A good source of **information** *(singular, general)* is the World Wide Web.

e **The information** *(singular, we know which information)* is on the company's website.

NOTE: we cannot say ~~an information~~, but we can say *a piece of information,* or *a source of information.*

> Which article *(the, a, an Ø)* do we use:
>
> 1 with single countable nouns referred to for the first time?
>
> 2 with plural countable nouns referred to for the first time?
>
> 3 with uncountable nouns?
>
> 4 when we refer to something already referred to or understood?

▶ **Grammar Reference page 159**

Pronunciation

1 ▭ 6.2 Listen to these sentences. How is *the* pronounced?

1 You can order at any time of the day.

2 The Internet offers you great choice.

3 It's *the* new way to shop.

2 Complete the sentences.

> **1** Before a consonant *the* is pronounced _____
>
> **2** Before a vowel *the* is pronounced _____
>
> **3** When it is stressed or emphatic *the* is pronounced _____

Language Practice

1 Are the nouns below countable or uncountable, singular or plural?

1 One in four **households** has a **computer**.

2 There are many **advantages** to buying on the Internet.

3 You can often find **products** on the Internet which are hard to find elsewhere.

4 All the **information** is up-to-date.

5 The **number** of Internet **users** in Latin America is growing fast.

6 **Europeans** show some resistance to **electronic commerce**.

7 There are some **problems**; if things go wrong, on-line **customers** in Tokyo cannot go to New York to get a refund.

2 Look at the title below. What sort of protection do you think is necessary?

3 Read the text. What are the advantages and disadvantages of Internet shopping?

4 Read the text again and put *a*, *an*, *the* or Ø in each gap.

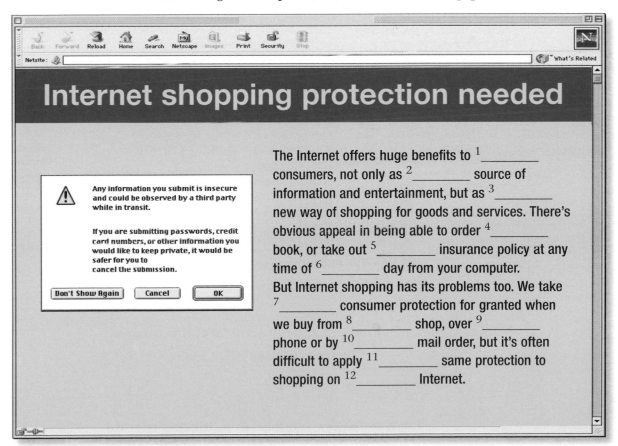

Internet shopping protection needed

⚠ Any information you submit is insecure and could be observed by a third party while in transit.

If you are submitting passwords, credit card numbers, or other information you would like to keep private, it would be safer for you to cancel the submission.

[Don't Show Again] [Cancel] [OK]

The Internet offers huge benefits to [1]_____ consumers, not only as [2]_____ source of information and entertainment, but as [3]_____ new way of shopping for goods and services. There's obvious appeal in being able to order [4]_____ book, or take out [5]_____ insurance policy at any time of [6]_____ day from your computer. But Internet shopping has its problems too. We take [7]_____ consumer protection for granted when we buy from [8]_____ shop, over [9]_____ phone or by [10]_____ mail order, but it's often difficult to apply [11]_____ same protection to shopping on [12]_____ Internet.

Reading

1 The text contains information about bar codes. Look at the sub heading. What information is contained in a bar code?

2 What other information do you think bar codes carry? Scan the text quickly and see if you are right.

Barcodes

Bars and stripes

Every time we go shopping at a supermarket, the price of each item is read from the barcode.

1 BAR CODES appear on just about everything we buy. They are patterns of thick and thin stripes, or bars, which an electronic scanner reads.

2 The stripes represent the 13-digit number underneath. An 8-digit bar code is used if there is not enough space on the packaging.

3 There are four main pieces of information on a bar code. The first two numbers represent the country in which the product was registered. This does not have to be the country of manufacture. The code for the UK and Ireland is 50. Some countries have three-digit codes: South Korea is 880 – to commemorate the 1988 Seoul Olympics.

4 Next comes the manufacturer's or supplier's code. Each manufacturer has a unique five-digit code. For example, Cadbury* is 00183, Nestlé* is 00243 and McVitie* is 00168.

The second group of five numbers represents the product and the package size, but not the price. The manufacturers can choose any number they want. Different producers can have the same number for their goods. 20389 might be a tube of toothpaste for one manufacturer and a tin of tomatoes for another. Bar codes also help shops with re-ordering. A shop's computer recognises the whole shape of a bar code when it passes across the scanner at a shop's checkout counter. It reads the bar code and the price of the product appears on the till display. At the same time one item is deducted from the stock total.

Security

6 Finally, the code finishes with a check digit that makes sure the bar code has been keyed in correctly. If not, the item will either not be recognised or will be shown as a totally different product.

COUNTRY CODES
Some examples of country codes are:

00-09	US and Canada
30-37	France
400-440	Germany
45,49	Japan
57	Denmark
80-83	Italy
93	Australia

There are also two special codes that take the place of country codes for the following:

977	Newspapers and magazines
978	Books

* *Cadbury:* chocolate manufacturer
* *Nestlé:* food manufacturer. Products include coffee and chocolate.
* *McVitie:* food manufacturer

The Guardian

9 780582 334540

3 Read the text carefully and label this barcode.

978   0582   33454   0

1 _____

2 _____

3 _____

4 _____

4 What do these numbers from the text refer to?

13   50   880   00183

Vocabulary Two

Word groups

1 Read the text again and underline these words.

barcode	packaging	manufacturer	checkout counter
till display	stock	supplier	price

Now complete the sentences.

1 A _____ is the pay desk in a self-service shop.

2 A _____ is a pattern of thick and thin lines that represents information.

3 A _____ is a firm which makes or produces goods.

4 A _____ is an electronic screen which shows you how much to pay.

5 A _____ is an agent who provides goods or services.

6 The _____ is used to protect goods and to present an image for them.

7 The _____ is the amount the goods cost.

8 The _____ is all the goods a retail outlet keeps to sell to its customers.

2 Find the phrases *tube of toothpaste* and *tin of tomatoes* in paragraph five of the text. These word partners describe how things are packaged.

Now match a package with a product.

Example:
a can of coke

milk

crisps

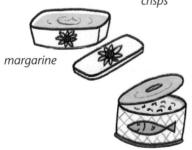

margarine

tuna fish

a carton of	1
a bag of	2
a packet of	3
a can of	4 cola
a bottle of	5
a tin of	6
a box of	7
a tub of	8
a jar of	9
a bar of	10

cigarettes

wine

cola

chocolate

chocolates

jam

3 Which nouns are uncountable?

4 Is the packaging for each item the same in your country? Do you have *cartons* of milk, for example?

Listening

1 Sarah Rochford talks about shopping at IKEA, a Swedish multinational. Read the statement by Goran Nilsson, Managing Director of IKEA, UK.

❝ We are proud of our home furnishing range and every one of our products has three important dimensions. Functional design, good quality materials and, most important of all, amazingly low prices. We call it Democratic Design. ❞

Before you listen say why you think Sarah likes shopping at IKEA.

2 ▭ 6.3 Listen and make notes about what Sarah says under these headings.

1 Frequency of visits to IKEA: _____

2 Opinion of IKEA products: _____

3 Opinion of IKEA stores: _____

4 Types of products she buys: _____

5 Aspects of shopping at IKEA she doesn't like: _____

6 Next trip: _____

3 Use your notes to write a list of advantages and disadvantages of shopping at IKEA. Then make a similar list for a store that you know.

Language Focus Two

Defining relative clauses

1 Defining relative clauses give important information about a noun. The clause is introduced by a relative pronoun *(which, that, who, where)*.

MAIN CLAUSE	RELATIVE PRONOUN	RELATIVE CLAUSE
A (bar code) is a pattern of thick and thin stripes	which	an electronic scanner reads.
The code finishes with a (check digit)	that	makes sure the bar code is correct.

2 🔲 6.4 Listen to six people talking about what is important to them when they shop. Match the different parts of the sentences.

Example:
I prefer sales assistants who let me look around by myself.

MAIN CLAUSE		RELATIVE CLAUSE	
1 I prefer sales assistants	who	**a**	have car parks.
2 I think it's important to have packaging	that	**b**	offer a wide variety of goods.
3 Because of the children, I need shops	which	**c**	put you under pressure and try to sell you things you don't want.
4 I like shops	that	**d**	clearly shows the ingredients.
5 I like shopping malls	where	**e**	all my favourite shops are in one place.
6 I don't like door-to-door salespeople	who	**f**	let me look around by myself.

3 What are the rules?

When the main clause is about:

1 a **person** or **people**, we introduce it with the relative pronoun _____ .

2 **things**, we introduce it with the relative pronoun _____ or *which*.

3 **places**, we introduce it with the relative pronoun _____ .

➤ **Grammar Reference page 156**

Packaging that clearly shows the ingredients

Language Practice

Add relative pronouns to the following sentences.

1 A retailer is a person _____ sells products to the customer in quantities _____ are convenient.

2 A retail outlet is a place _____ customers can purchase the goods.

3 A supermarket is a store _____ sells a wide variety of goods.

4 A 'middleman' is a person _____ makes a profit by selling goods for more than he/she paid for them.

5 A speciality store is a retail outlet _____ sells a particular type of goods.

Writing

Expanding notes

Use the notes below to write a short magazine article about retailing.

- Begin with a description of the current situation.

- Add two paragraphs describing the advantages and disadvantages of home shopping and traditional shopping.

Be careful with articles and use relative clauses to make your writing fluent!

Home Shopping & Traditional Shopping

- 40% shoppers interested in weekly delivery service for foodstuffs and household goods

- 75% like stores open early & late

- Many supermarkets planning catalogue/home delivery/electronic ordering

- Consumer protection difficult to regulate on the Internet

- Many traditional shoppers happy with current situation

- Traditional shopping – can see, touch, smell the goods

- Going to the shops – buy goods, have the goods immediately

- TV shopping and Internet shopping popular

You could start like this:

Home shopping habits are changing. In the past consumers usually bought products direct from the supermarket, from local shop or from a department store. Now...

Business Communication

Telephoning

1 When you make a phone call to a person in company, you often have to call a switchboard or general number first then ask the receptionist for the person you want to speak to.

Here are some expressions to help you get through.

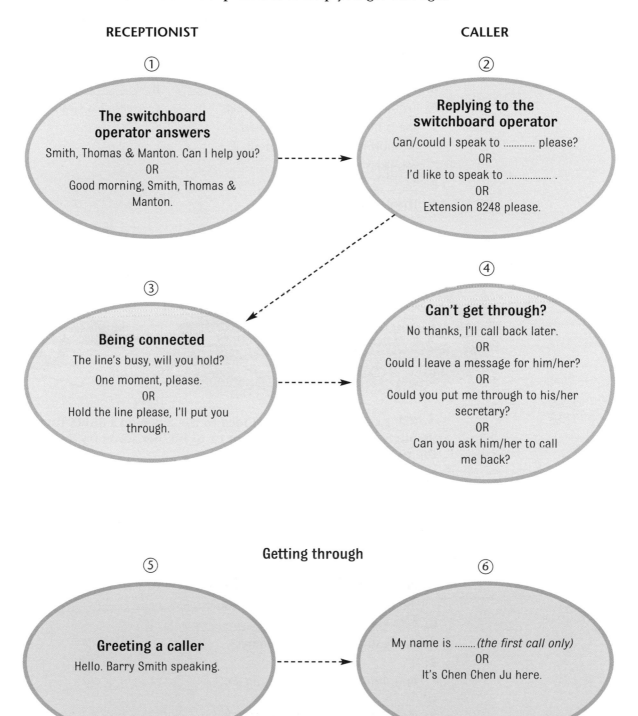

RECEPTIONIST   CALLER

①
The switchboard operator answers
Smith, Thomas & Manton. Can I help you?
OR
Good morning, Smith, Thomas & Manton.

②
Replying to the switchboard operator
Can/could I speak to .... please?
OR
I'd like to speak to ....
OR
Extension 8248 please.

③
Being connected
The line's busy, will you hold?
One moment, please.
OR
Hold the line please, I'll put you through.

④
Can't get through?
No thanks, I'll call back later.
OR
Could I leave a message for him/her?
OR
Could you put me through to his/her secretary?
OR
Can you ask him/her to call me back?

Getting through

⑤
Greeting a caller
Hello. Barry Smith speaking.

⑥
My name is ....*(the first call only)*
OR
It's Chen Chen Ju here.

2 🔲 6.5 **Look at the two conversations below. What do you think the people say? Write in your guess then listen and check your answers.**

THROUGH THE SWITCHBOARD

Conversation 1

A: Good morning, Dunton Associates

B: Oh hello, ¹_____

A: Just one moment.
I'm afraid Ms Holt's line is busy.

B: ²_____

A: Just one moment. I'm afraid that
line is busy, too. I can put you
through to the message desk, if
you like.

B: ³_____

A: Thank you. Goodbye.

Conversation 2

A: Smith, Thomas and Manton.

B: ⁴_____
It's ringing for you.

C: Hello, Barry Smith speaking.

B: ⁵_____

C: Hello, Ms Grant.

3 🔲 6.6 **It's always a good idea to use a person's direct line; you will get through to the person you want or to his/her secretary. Listen and complete the two conversations.**

DIRECT LINE

Conversation 1

A: Hello, Joanna Coutts. How may I
help you?

B: ¹_____?

A: I'm afraid she's out of the office at the
moment. Can I get her to call you?

B: ²_____

A: Can you give me your number?

B: ³_____
And, I'm sorry, your name again.

B: ⁴_____

A: OK Ms Parry, I'll ask her to call you.

B: Thank you.

A: Thank you. Goodbye.

B: Goodbye.

Conversation 2

A: Hello, Pat Summers.

B: ⁵_____

A: Hello Chris. How are you?

B: Fine thanks …

4 Work in groups of three. Student A is a telephone operator, Student B is a caller, and Student C is the person the caller wants to speak to. Take it in turns to practise the opening sentences of a phone call.

5 Change groups. Practise the opening sentences of a phone call again.

Final Task   1 Work in pairs. Choose a shop you both know, then read the rolecards.

STUDENT A

You are the Shop Manager. Student B is a customer. Telephone Student B to find out what he/she thinks about shopping at your store. You want to find out what customers think so that you can improve your service. You have a lot of competition from home shopping and want to stay competitive. Use the headings from the **Listening** section (page 62) to help you get the information you need.

STUDENT B

You are a customer and your partner is the Shop Manager. He/She telephones you to ask about your experience of shopping at the store. Answer his/her questions truthfully and use this opportunity to tell him/her about changes you think are necessary. You find home shopping very convenient, so you think traditional stores need to change to adapt to the market.

2 Have the telephone conversation.

Checklist for Unit 6:

[ ] 1 Name five different types of retail outlet.

[ ] 2 Name five forms of direct selling.

[ ] 3 Give one advantage and one disadvantage of shopping on the Internet.

[ ] 4 What information do bar codes contain? Why are they important?

[ ] 5 Which of these nouns can we use the indefinite article with? Why?
   margarine   *information*   *Internet*   *retail outlet*

[ ] 6 What do you say when you phone a company and ask to speak to someone?

Troubleshooting, Company History and Retailing

Business Review

1 Read about Selfridges.

Selfridges is a department store which began trading over 85 years ago. It is based in Oxford Street and is London's second largest department store after Harrods, with 150,000m² of retail space. In the 1990s the store experienced some problems with its image because people thought it was old-fashioned. To solve the problem, Selfridges invested £50m to re-establish the business as one of the capital's main shopping attractions. They decided to offer a wide choice of products to attract more customers. They built a huge central 'atrium' or entrance hall, and a series of new stores. Some of the stores are re-designed and others, such as Children's World, have their own restaurant.

1 Describe the store: age, location, size and what type of retail outlet it is.

2 Who is its main competitor?

3 What problem did the store have?

4 What troubleshooting strategy did they use to solve the problem?

5 What new features does the store offer?

6 Underline *one* example of a defining relative clause, *two* clauses of purpose and *three* regular past tense verbs.

2 Work in pairs. Choose one company from each unit then use the prompts to write three short paragraphs.

- IMG and Ford - **Troubleshooting** (*prompt* - situation? solution?)

- M&S, Bic and EMI - **Company History** (*prompt* - key events in company history)

- IKEA - **Retailing** (*prompt* - product design, quality, price)

3 Exchange paragraphs with another pair. Give them one point for each piece of correct information. Which pair in the group has the most points?

Vocabulary Review

The words below are all from the key vocabulary sections of units 4, 5 and 6.

Match each word to the correct definition.
Example: *1c*

VOCABULARY	
1 strategy	7 services
2 SWOT analysis	8 retail outlet
3 troubleshooting	9 profit margin
4 established	10 supermarket
5 founder	11 'remote' shopping
6 goods	12 mail order

DEFINITION
a founded
b jobs where people do or provide something rather than produce something
c plan
d shopping from home by choosing goods from a company's catalogue
e the person who started the company
f an analysis of a company's situation
g solving problems
h shopping from home via the Internet or by TV shopping channel
i shop
j the difference between how much it costs to produce goods and the price the consumer pays for them
k a large self-service shop selling different brands of everyday goods
l products

Grammar Review

Read the advertisement and fill the gaps.
Paragraph 1: use these verbs in the past simple:

to open   to begin   to become

Paragraph 2: use *the, a(n) or Ø.*
Paragraph 3: use *should/ought to.*

Sales Assistants

① We are a large department store which
¹_____ trading in 1895. Our famous
textiles department ²_____ in 1920 and
quickly ³_____ very popular.

② We are looking for ⁴_____ motivated Sales
Assistants to work within ⁵_____ variety of
departments around ⁶_____ store. These
positions are available for ⁷_____ one
year.

③ The ideal candidate ⁸_____ have at least 6
to 12 months' experience of working in a retail
environment, and ⁹_____ be familiar with
department stores. These roles are very
demanding and applicants ¹⁰_____ be
committed and hard-working.

④ If you are interested in the above positions,
please call in to our Recruitment Centre for
an application form.

Defining relative clauses

**1 Match a main clause in box A with the
correct relative clause in box B.**

Example: *3b*

A
1	A management consultant is a person
2	Ford is a company
3	Bic is a company
4	A shopping centre is a place
5	Bar codes are a pattern of stripes

B
a	produces disposable products
b	customers can find many different shops
c	gives advice to companies
d	an electronic scanner reads
e	manufactures cars

**2 Write six sentences using the correct relative
pronoun (*who, that, which, where*).**

Example: *A management consultant is a person
who gives advice to companies.*

Writing Review

**1 You are halfway through *First Insights Into
Business*. Think about your progress, and
evaluate your strengths and weaknesses in
English. Complete a SWOT analysis for yourself.**

**2 Now look at the table and complete a similar
one using the information from your SWOT
analysis.**

Weaknesses/threats
1 I find it difficult to remember the past tense
of irregular verbs.
2

Recommendation
1 I should look at the verb list and do the
workbook exercises in Unit 5.
2

Purpose
1 To help remember the forms and use them
correctly.
2

Business Communication Review

**Work in pairs. Student A look at the
information below. Student B see page 149.**

STUDENT A

You want to speak to the Head of Sales at Bond
& Co., a company which manufactures silk ties,
because you want to stock their ties in your
department store. You telephone the company.
The Head of Sales is not in his office so you leave
a message with Student B, a Sales Representative.

• Explain who you are and who you would like
to speak to.
• Give a brief presentation of your company.
• Explain that you would like to stock Bond &
Co's ties in your store.

Prepare the call, then telephone your partner.
Try to 'sell' a positive image of your company.

In this unit:

- **Language Focus**
  Order of adjectives
  Comparative and superlative adjectives
  Pronunciation: weak forms /ə/ /ɪst/, /ðən/, /əz/

- **Skills**
  Writing: linking words of cause and effect
  Reading: Dyson product launch
  Listening: advertising products

- **Vocabulary**
  Word partners, word building

- **Business Communication**
  Product presentation

Key Vocabulary

🔲 **7.1** For nearly every type of **product** there are many similar goods on the market. The **unique selling points (USPs)** of a product are the things that make it special and different from other similar products. A good **advertisement**, which brings the product to the public's attention, should describe these USPs. The marketing department should have a **customer profile** in mind, that is the sort of person who will buy the product. When trying to sell a product, it's important to give information about the product's **features** or characteristics, and to emphasise the **benefits** or advantages of the product to the customer.

Lead-in

aerobic workout machine

2000-file organiser with PC data link

portable CD player

no battery solar watch

1 🔲 **7.2 Listen to part of a sales presentation for one of the products above. Which product is it?**

2 Work in pairs. For each product discuss the following.

- What are the features of the product?
- What are the product's benefits to the customer. What are the USPs?
- What type of customer probably buys this product?

3 Which of the products would you like to own and why?

Language Focus One

Order of adjectives

1 Label the briefcase using the words below.

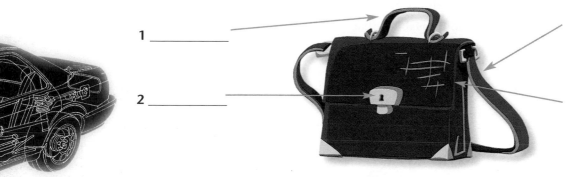

A stylish durable leather briefcase with convenient long, wide carrying strap.

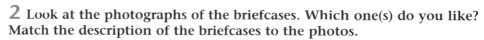

| lock | trim | shoulder strap | handle |

2 Look at the photographs of the briefcases. Which one(s) do you like? Match the description of the briefcases to the photos.

a an unusual sporty briefcase with practical nylon straps and black trim

b an elegant light brown briefcase with brass locks

c a styish leather briefcase with a beautiful glass handle

d a durable leather briefcase with brass locks

e an Italian black leather briefcase with a long shoulder strap

3 Which adjectives in exercise 2 give opinions and which give facts?

Example: **opinion** – *stylish, beautiful*
fact – *leather, glass*

4 For each of the briefcases, complete the table with words from the sentences under these headings.

①

②

③

④

⑤

OPINION	FACT					
	size/ length	shape/ width	colour	where it's from	what it's made of	
① *stylish*					*leather*	briefcase
beautiful					*glass*	handle
②						briefcase
						straps
						trim
③						briefcase
						strap
④						briefcase
						locks
⑤						briefcase
						locks

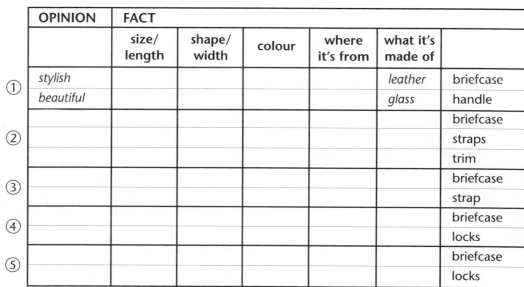

5 Now add these three descriptions to the table.

1 a big, square, leather folder

2 a large, extra-wide sports bag

3 a spacious, oval handbag

6 Use all the sentences to answer these questions.

> **1** Do 'opinion' adjectives usually go before or after 'fact' adjectives?
>
> **2** 'Fact' adjectives usually go in this order:
> size, _____ , _____ , _____ , _____
>
> **3** Do 'size' and 'length' adjectives (e.g. big, small, long, short) usually go before or after 'shape' and 'width' adjectives (e.g. slim, fat, narrow, wide, broad)?
>
> Now look at the Grammar Reference to check your answers.

▶ **Grammar Reference page 158**

Language Practice One

1 Work in pairs. Choose three of the products from the photographs below and write down three adjectives to describe each one. Use adjectives from the box and any others you can think of.

expensive	useful	smart	practical	beautiful
fun	stylish	colourful	top-of-the-range	

2 Now put the adjectives in the correct order.

3 Work in pairs. Find four products (e.g. glasses, bags, clothes, jewellery). Write a list of adjectives to describe each one, and put them in the correct order. Give your list to another pair for them to identify the product.

Reading

James Dyson – inventor

1 Look at the Dyson vacuum cleaners and answer the questions.

1 How are these Dyson products different from most vacuum cleaners?

2 Who is the target customer for this product in your opinion?

2 Which words describe these vacuum cleaners?

crazy	dull	eye-catching	fun
innovative	stylish	old-fashioned	traditional
high quality	reliable	high performance	

3 Read what the Dyson company literature says about this product. Why are the colours grey and yellow used? Are they effective?

❝ *The silver-grey body, like machined aluminium, resembles a piece of aircraft technology. Yellow is used to highlight the important parts and give it a sense of fun.* ❞

4 Read the extract from the brochure and say what these figures refer to.

a 1978   **b** 5   **c** 5,127   **d** 23

▶ In 1978 James Dyson had an idea for inventing new vacuum cleaning technology. It was the same year that his third child, Sam, was born.

▶ 5 long years and 5,127 prototypes* later, this idea became a working model.

▶ It was another 10 years before it began to be manufactured under his own name. By this time, both Sam and his invention were 15 years old.

▶ Just 23 months after launch* in the UK, his invention became Britain's best-selling vacuum cleaner, overtaking sales of Hoover, Electrolux, Panasonic, Miele and all other vacuum cleaners.

* *prototype:* an example design produced for testing
* *launch:* putting a new product on the market

Doing a Dyson

5 **Work in pairs and discuss these questions.**

1 How long did it take to launch the product? Do you think this is normal?

2 Why do you think there were so many prototypes?

3 Who are Dyson's main competitors?

4 How successful is his business today?

6 **Now quickly read a magazine article about James Dyson's product.**

1 What did Dyson win and why?

2 What *doesn't* the Dyson vacuum cleaner have?

3 Where did Dyson get backing (money) for his invention? Why didn't he get it in Britain?

James Dyson

the man who launched a multi-million pound business with a new type of vacuum cleaner, won the European Design Prize last night.

"I am absolutely delighted," said Mr Dyson. "... to win the award for something that uses technology rather than something that just looks good."

Mr Dyson's vacuum cleaner marked the biggest change in the battle against house dust since Hubert Cecil Booth, a Scot, invented the first 'suction cleaner' in 1901.

Dyson's appliance* does not use bags to collect dust.

Mr Dyson, who trained in interior design at the Royal College of Art, invented the machine in the 1980s by converting an old vacuum cleaner using pieces of swimming pool hose.

British firms turned him down so the inventor had to go to the United States and Japan to get backing. "That is the British disease I'm afraid." he said. "We have a 'can't do' attitude, whereas many of our competitors are much more aware of the importance of innovation*." But he also had to fight in the American courts to stop others stealing* his idea. This award shows how important design is — the company had a turnover of zero pounds three years ago and has a turnover of £100 million today.

* *appliance:* piece of electrical equipment
* *innovation:* creating new inventions or ideas
* *to steal:* to take something without permission

The Guardian

7 **The following sentences tell us about five different events in the development process. Put them in the correct chronological sequence.**

a Dyson won the European Design Prize last night. ☐

b Hubert Cecil Booth invented the first vacuum or 'suction' cleaner in 1901. 1

c Dyson studied at the Royal College of Art. ☐

d He went to the United States and Japan for development backing. ☐

e The company had a turnover of zero pounds three years ago. ☐

Vocabulary

Word partners

1 Underline the following words in the text then match a verb and a noun to make word partners.

VERB	NOUN
to get	a machine
to steal	a prize
to invent	an idea
to win	backing

2 Complete the sentences with word partners from the box above. Be careful with the tense.

1 He _____ _____ for best designer of the year.

2 In 1901 Cecil Booth _____ _____. It was called a 'suction cleaner'.

3 Dyson didn't want people to _____ his _____ before he launched the vacuum cleaner.

4 Developing the vacuum cleaner was an expensive process, so Dyson needed to _____ _____ to complete the project.

Word building

3 Complete the table using words from the text.

VERB	NOUN	NOUN PERSON
to award	1 _____	
2 _____	invention	3 _____
4 _____	development	5 _____
innovate	6 _____	innovator
compete	competition	7 _____

4 Use one of the forms to complete the sentences.

1 All inventors are _____ because they are creating something new.

2 The _____ of the computer changed the way we work.

3 It can take years to research and _____ new drugs.

4 There were hundreds of first class companies to consider, so they were delighted to win the _____ against such strong _____ .

Writing

Linking words of cause and effect

1 Read the following sentences and notice how the linking words are used.

Cause

1 Most vacuum cleaners lose up to 50% of their power **because** the bag becomes blocked.

2 **As/Since** the Dyson vacuum cleaners don't have bags, they are very efficient.

> *Because*, *as* and *since* link cause and effect within one sentence.

Effect

1 British firms turned him down. **As a result** he had to go to the United States and Japan to get backing.

2 British firms turned him down **so** the inventor had to go to the United States and Japan to get backing.

3 British firms turned him down. He **therefore** had to go to the United States and Japan to get backing.

> *As a result* and *therefore* link two sentences. *So* links cause and effect within one sentence.

2 Link sentences *a* and *b* below using a linking word of *either* cause *or* effect.

Example:
a The product is faulty.
b The manufacturers are withdrawing the product from the shops.

EITHER: *The manufacturers are withdrawing the product from the shops* **because** *it is faulty.*

OR: *The product is faulty.* **Therefore** *the manufacturers are withdrawing it from the shops.*

1 **a** The cost of raw materials increased.

   b The price of manufactured goods also increased.

2 **a** All the manufacturers refused to back the design.

   b The inventor produced the new vacuum cleaner himself.

3 **a** The product is not selling well.

   b We need to change our marketing strategy.

4 **a** The company set the price of the product too high.

   b Demand was low.

▶ **Grammar Reference page 157**

Language Focus Two

Comparative and superlative adjectives: making comparisons

Read the descriptions of the menswear collections.

IL CLASSICO	**Allegro**	**SHERRINGTON**
$525 to $705	$525 to $685	$645 to $1,300
The classic business look for the man who is fashionably discreet.	Softer lines, informal, and relaxed for the man interested in fashion.	Top quality, hand-crafted in Italy for the man who can afford whatever he wants.

Now read these sentences and complete the grammar rules.

1 To compare two items: **comparative adjectives**

*The Sherrington collection is **more expensive than** the Allegro collection.*

*The Allegro collection has **softer lines than** the Il Classico collection.*

a Adjectives with one syllable (e.g. *cheap*) add _____ to the adjective.

b Adjectives with more than one syllable (e.g. *expensive*) add _____ or _____ before the adjective.

c Use _____ before the second item to connect the items.

2 To compare **more than two** items: **superlative adjectives**

*Of the three different collections, the Sherrington collection is the most **expensive** and the Il Classico collection is **the least expensive**.*

*All the clothes are very good quality, but the Sherrington collection is of **the highest quality**.*

a Adjectives with one syllable (e.g. *high*) add _____ before the adjective and add _____ to the end of the adjective.

b Adjectives with more than one syllable (e.g. *expensive*) add _____ _____ or _____ _____ before the adjective.

3 Clauses of comparison

*The Allegro collection is **not as expensive as** the Sherrington collection.*

*Some of the Allegro collection is **as expensive as** the Sherrington collection.*

Use (not) _____ + adj. + _____ to compare two items.

4 Negative Comparison

*The Allegro is **less expensive than** the Sherrington collection.*

5 Irregular adjectives

good   better   the best   bad   worse   the worst

► **Grammar Reference page 158**

Pronunciation

🔲 7.3 **Comparative and superlative endings /ə/ and /əst/**

1 Listen to these adjectives. Notice how *-er* and *-est* are pronounced.

soft	softer	softest
smart	smarter	smartest

2 🔲 7.4 Listen and repeat these comparative and superlative forms.

1 soft lines	**2** smart suit	**3** sharp lines	**4** cool suit
5 warm suit	**6** light fabric	**7** heavy fabric	

Weak forms: than /ðən/, as /əz/

3 🔲 7.5 Listen and notice how *than* and *as* are pronounced.

1 This suit is more expensive *than* that suit.

2 This briefcase is less expensive *than* that briefcase.

3 These suits are *as* expensive *as* those suits.

4 The Allegro collection isn't *as* expensive *as* the Il Classico collection.

4 Work in pairs. Practise saying the sentences in Language Focus Two.

Language Practice Two

1 Work in pairs. Look at the chart showing *the* colour preferences of luxury car owners. Write five sentences of comparison.

Example:
1 White is the most popular colour.

2 Work in pairs. Choose three of the products below and think of two different brands for each. Compare the brands.

- perfumes/after-shaves
- cars
- dictionaries
- soft drinks
- cigarettes
- newspapers/magazines
- training shoes
- jeans

Example:
Chanel No. 5 is more expensive than Eau de Lâncome, and it is also more popular, but I prefer Eau de Lâncome because it is lighter.

TOP TEN LUXURY CAR COLOURS

Luxury car-owners like white – but green is getting hot.

Colour	Market share
1. White	21.57%
2. Silver	10.25%
3. Medium red	9.84%
4. Light brown	9.75%
5. Green	7.55%
6. Light blue	6.75%
7. Black	6.42%
8. Dark blue	6.34%
9. Medium grey	5.82%
10. Dark red	3.86%

3 Change partners and find out your partner's preferences.

Listening

1 **Verena Adams is going to talk about the role of advertising in selling products. Before you listen, work in pairs and discuss the following points.**

Verena mentions two types of product: *fast moving consumer goods* (fmcgs) and *consumer durables*. Which type of product:

1 does the consumer buy often and use quickly?

2 does the consumer buy occasionally?

3 is more expensive?

2 **Which category do these items belong to?**

shoes	clothes	beer	cars	canned drinks
computers	CD players	chocolate	wine	fruit
envelopes	compact discs	televisions	meat	washing machines

3 **Make a list of different types of advertisements, and say which ones are used for *fmcgs* and which ones for *consumer durables*?**

Example: *TV adverts – consumer durables e.g. cars, and fmcgs e.g. chocolate.*

4 🔲 **7.6 Listen and answer the questions.**

1 How does Verena Adams describe advertising? Complete the sentence:

Advertising is a _____, it can work in different ways.

2 What are the four ways in which advertising can work?

3 Make notes about how to advertise Tango, (a soft drink), and a car.

	Tango	a car
Target audience	a _____	not given
Design of advertisement	eye-catching and b_____	press ads with details of c_____ _____
Style of campaign	crazy d_____ _____	not given
Media	Television	Press ads and e_____ as back-up
Purpose of advertisement	to motivate the market to buy	to f_____

4 What is the function of the advertising agency?

5 What makes a good advertisement in Verena's opinion?

Business Communication

Product presentation

1 ▭ **7.7 Listen to the sales presentation of the new video phone and choose the correct answer.**

1 What is the name of the product?
a ViTa Desktop Videophone
b ViaTV Desktop Videophone
c Via Desktop Videophone

2 The salesperson describes the product as
a small and slim
b small and attractive
c small and elegant

3 To set up the product you need
a a touch-tone phone
b a computer
c special software

4 Which special feature does the salesperson *not* mention?
a full colour-motion video
b on-screen menus
c very good picture quality
d preview mode
e privacy mode

5 In order to see the person you are calling
a you need the product
b the caller needs the product
c both parties need the product

2 ▭ **7.7 Listen again. What benefit does the salesperson emphasise? Who is the target customer, in your opinion?**

3 Use the answers to complete the summary.

Name: The full name of the product is [1] _____.

Appearance: It is [2] _____.

User-friendliness: It is easy to set up – all you need is [3] _____.

Special features: The special features include [4] _____.
in addition it has [5] _____.

Benefits: The main benefit of the product is [6] _____.

4 Work in two groups. Read the information about your product and complete the summary.

Group A: Look at the advertisement for the multi-lingual European interpreter on page 81. Read the advertisement and complete the summary.

❝ *With the multi-lingual European interpreter you will never be lost for words. Make your business trips easier and more enjoyable.* ❞

Group B: Look at the advertisement for the Memo Recording Pen on page 148.

Your multi-lingual European interpreter

This electronic interpreter is fluent in 7 languages (English, German, Spanish, French, Italian, Dutch and Swedish) with a working knowledge of over 30,000 words in each language. It includes an automatic spelling correction so you can input foreign words phonetically, a 30-entry name/address databank, full function calculator, metric and currency converters and word games. Batteries supplied.

7-language translator £49.95

Appearance: stylish and compact

Benefits: _____

_____

_____

Price: _____

Special features:

• _____ languages

• _____ words per language

• _____

• 30 entry _____

• _____

• _____

• word games

---

5 In your groups prepare a sales presentation on your product. Use the summary notes in exercise 3 to help you.

Find a partner from the other group and give your presentation. Be enthusiastic and convince your partner to buy your product.

Final Task

Speaking

Think of a product you would like to buy.

• Describe the customer profile.

• Describe its features and benefits.

• Give reasons for the benefits (use linking words of cause and effect).

Checklist for Unit 7:

☐ 1 Put the following adjectives in order to make a product description.
   leather   blue   smart   slim   briefcase

☐ 2 What are the comparative and superlative forms of these adjectives?
   reliable   expensive   soft   light   new   stylish

☐ 3 Compare a BMW and a Skoda.

☐ 4 Choose three products from this unit. What are the features of each?

☐ 5 What are the benefits of each feature?

8 *People*

Key Vocabulary

8.1 Most people work because they need to earn a **salary**, but money is not the only **motivation** or reason why people work. People get **job satisfaction** from different factors, such as **social interaction** with colleagues. **Status**, that is your professional position, and **achievement**, doing something well, can be important. Some companies really value their employees and see them as the company's main **asset**. Managing people well can lead to better results and **higher productivity** for the company, but this can be difficult to do. People respond differently to different **styles of management**. Some organisations give their workers freedom to develop their roles and others don't.

Lead-in

Look at the survey below, then choose six factors which are important for you. Compare them with a partner.

Factors considered when choosing your first job

I want to:	% of graduates	I want to:	% of graduates
enjoy my job	72	be passionate about the industry I work in	30
like the people I work with	70	have job security*	30
have enough money to afford the things I enjoy	64	be in control of what I do	27
receive training	63	have a lot of freedom at work	21
find the work stimulating	57	work for a well-known company	18
have an inspirational* boss	41	not have to work overtime or at weekends	17
have a good social life	40	have a job that will take me abroad	16
have the opportunity to take professional qualifications	39	have an excellent salary	15
work for a respected* company	35	have other people think what I do sounds good	11
have a position of responsibility	30		

inspirational: motivating   *respected*: people think well of [the company]   *job security*: no worry about losing your job

Cross-cultural Communication

" *Managers have to learn how to be teachers, counsellors and friends ...* "

Charles Handy (Management specialist)

Work in pairs and discuss these questions.

1 Do you agree with Handy's view?

2 What is the main role of managers in companies in your country?

3 How much control should employees have over their own work ?

4 How much should the manager control what the employee does?

Language Focus One

Going to for future plans and intentions

1 ▭ 8.2 Dan Goldman has a performance appraisal with his line manager, Philippa Taylor. They discuss his performance since the last meeting and set targets for the next meeting in six months' time. Listen and complete Philippa's notes.

Appraisee's performance in the past six months

Dan is getting on well.
He is ¹_____ the work.
Particularly pleased with ²_____ .

Areas where appraisee needs to improve

1. Time management

Action to improve performance in these areas
Intentions
He's going to ³_____ .
He going to ⁴_____ .

Definite:
He's doing a course next month.
Scott Henman ⁵_____ the course.

Compare your notes with a partner.

2 **In the second part of the interview Dan talks about:**

a his future plans and intentions and   b a definite future arrangement

Which tense does he use for each?

3 **True or false?**

We use *going to* to talk about something we really want or intend to do in the future.

▶ **Grammar Reference page 151**

Pronunciation One

🔲 **8.2b Weak forms of *to* /tə/**

1 Listen to Dan talking about how he intends to improve his time management skills.

Notice how *to* is pronounced when Dan says:

> 1 I'm going to try to prioritise more.
>
> 2 I'm going to set myself more realistic deadlines.

2 🔲 **8.3 Listen and repeat these questions.**

1 When are you going *to* spend time in an English-speaking country?

2 What time are you going *to* leave today?

3 What are you going *to* do this evening?

4 When are you going *to* apply for a new job?

5 What type of job are you going *to* apply for?

3 Work in pairs. Ask and answer the questions in exercise 2.

Language Practice One

Juan

1 Work in pairs. Juan, Aleka and Chan each have a different objective. They write a list of action points to meet their objective. Decide which points belong to which person.

> **Objectives**
> - Chan: spend more time with my family
> - Aleka: buy a new computer because I want to work from home
> - Juan: get a new job

Action points

1 buy magazines to get more information

2 talk to a careers consultant

3 consider what gives me job satisfaction

4 decide exactly what I need and find a product that matches my needs

5 do research to see what jobs and companies match my values

6 leave work earlier

7 not take work home at the weekends

8 start work earlier

9 talk to people who have different kinds of computers

2 Now write sentences to describe Juan, Aleka and Chan's intentions.
Example:
*Chan is **going to** leave work earlier **to spend** more time with his family.*

3 Now think of three objectives which are important to you and write an action plan to reach each objective.

Compare your objectives and action plan with a partner.

Chan

Language Focus Two

Will for the future

1 Read the recruitment advertisement and answer these questions.

1 Who is advertising?
2 Who do they want to recruit?
3 What is the name of the programme they want the recruits to join?
4 What is the main quality they are looking for?

Graduates/Final Year students

Priceless training.

free thinking.

Bring us free thinking and we'll give you invaluable training for a unique career.

Our 4 year Fast Stream Programme will give you an insight into the development of government policy, the complexities of tax law and practice, and how a major organisation is managed. You will learn how different types of business operate and develop your skills so that you can take on the wide range of career opportunities we offer.

Determined, with excellent interpersonal and communication skills, a strong analytical mind and the confidence to make critical decisions, you'll need the drive and self-discipline to take on growing responsibilities and demanding exams at the same time. You'll also need to have, or be expecting, a first or second class honours degree, and be free to join us in July in London or a range of locations in southern England and the Midlands.

In return, as well as exceptional training, you can expect a starting salary between around £14,000 and £21,000 depending on location, qualifications and experience. If you meet our expectations you can expect to be earning £30,000 in 4 years.

Only your potential counts with us. We are firmly committed to recruit, develop and promote people on their abilities, and will not discriminate on grounds of gender or race.

For further information and an application form, write to Inland Revenue, Fast Stream Development Programme, HR Division, PO Box 55, Mowbray House, Castle Meadow Road, Nottingham, NG2 1BE quoting reference FS/G2. Telephone 01150974 0696. We must have your completed application form by 6 November.

 The Inland Revenue is an Equal Opportunities Employer.

2 Read the advertisement again and complete the sentences with a verb.

1 We will _____ you invaluable training for a unique career.
2 The Fast Stream Programme will _____ you insight into government policy.
3 You will _____ how different types of business operate.
4 You will _____ drive and self-discipline.
5 We will not _____ on grounds of gender or race.
6 They _____ accept applications after 6 November.

Pronunciation Two

Short form of *will*

1 📼 8.4 Listen and notice how the speaker pronounces *will* in these sentences. Repeat the sentences.

2 The six sentences from Language Focus exercise 2 describe working for the Inland Revenue in the future. Look at the sentences. Are the following true or false?

a We use *will* to talk generally about the future.	T/F
b *Will* is always followed by infinitive without to.	T/F
c The negative is formed: *will* + *not* + **infinitive without** *to*.	T/F
d In the written form will is often written *'ll*.	T/F
e The short form of *will/will* **not** is always used in speaking except in questions and short answers. e.g. *Will* you give me training? Yes, we *will*.	T/F

► **Grammar Reference page 151**

Language Practice Two

1 Use these prompts to write six sentences.
Example:
Inland Revenue/give/training
Inland Revenue will give you training.

1 You/learn/management skills
2 we/offer/excellent training
3 you/earn/£14,000 – £21,000 per year
4 you/take/exams
5 Inland Revenue/not/discriminate against you
6 you/live/Southern England

2 Now say the sentences. Remember to use the short form of *will*.

3 Work in pairs.
Student A You see the following advertisement. Phone your partner to find out more.
Student B turn to page 148.

Fantastic Job Opportunity In IT

Phone +44 171 92000954 to find out more.

STUDENT A

Phone Student B to find out about this job.

Use the future form *will* to ask Student B for information. Ask about:

• opportunities to use my languages?
• work abroad?
• receive training?
• date of interviews? (*When* ...?)

Example:
Will I have opportunities to use my languages?

Listening

1 🖭 8.5 **Morna Lawson talks about various aspects of work. Listen and complete the notes.**

Job satisfaction

1 Three things that are important to Morna in a job: _____

_____

Management styles

2 She likes a manager to be ª_____ , but at the same time to be
ᵇ_____. In other words the manager allows her to get on with it,
but is there to ᶜ_____ her.

Workplace culture

3 Spain and Britain are probably similar now, but when Morna worked in Spain she
noticed that _____ .

Managers

4 Morna's favourite manager was ª_____. She allowed her to get on
with the work and to ᵇ_____ (it wasn't the end of the world) and
Morna ᶜ_____.

Work in pairs and compare your notes.

2 **How would you like your manager to be? Choose three descriptions.**

| supportive | hands-off | available |
| a good teacher | understanding | inspirational |

3 **Morna talks about the workplace cultures in Britain and Spain.
Look at your notes and choose a sentence that matches what she says.**

①

②

a The Spanish live to work and the British work to live.

b The British live to work and the Spanish work to live.

What is the workplace culture in your country like?

Reading

1 The text is about the different styles that men and women have in the workplace. Look at the cartoons and say which figures you think represent men and which represent women?

(a)

confrontational, competitive

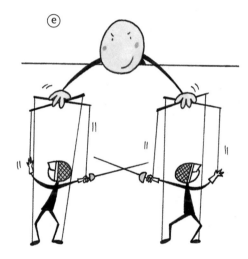

(b)

personal achievement comes first

(c)

share credit for success

(d)

forceful, self-protective, challenging, direct

(e)

in control

(f)

collaborative

(g)

welcome contributions

(h)

How's your daughter?

talk about personal matters

(i)

hysterical

2 Read the text and see if the writer's ideas are the same as yours.

3 The text has eight main sub-sections. Match the cartoons on page 88 to the sections.

MEN and women do things differently. There are, of course, exceptions to every generalisation, including this one.

Cristina Stuart is a managing director of Speakeasy Training, a consultancy that runs courses for men and women working together. Here she describes a few key differences between the sexes in the workplace.

1 Working together
The male approach to business is competitive, direct and confrontational. The end justifies the means.* Personal status and a focus on the individual are important.

The female method is collaborative. Collective action and responsibility are more important than personal achievement. Lateral thinking*, as well as goodwill and the well-being of the individual, are also of great importance.

2 Tackling problems
The male approach is to go to the heart of the problem, without taking into account secondary considerations. The female preference is to look at various options.

3 Body language
Male body language tends to be challenging. Female body language tends towards self-protection. A stereotypical female pose is sitting cross-legged; the male sits with legs apart to give an impression that he is in control.

Male behaviour can include forceful gestures for example banging a fist on the desk for effect. The female style does not usually include aggressive gestures.

4 Language
The male way of speaking does not encourage discussion. Women tend to welcome others' opinions and contributions more.

5 Conversation
Men like to talk about their personal experiences and achievements or discuss 'masculine' topics such as cars or sport. Women tend to talk about staff problems and personal matters.

6 Meetings
If a woman does not copy the male confrontational style, she is often ignored.

7 Self-promotion
Men find it easy to tell others about their successes. Women tend to share or pass on the credit for a success.

8 Humour
Men's humour can be cruel – a man's joke usually has a victim. Female humour is less hurtful. A woman often jokes against herself.

CAVEAT
Many men have a female style of working. Equally many women have a male approach.

As Ms Stuart says many of the current management theorems – flatter organisations*, empowerment, managing by consensus* – have a female style to them.

* *the end justifies the means:* it doesn't matter what methods you use; success is the only important thing
* *lateral thinking:* thinking in a creative way, making unusual connections
* *flatter organisations:* organisations in which there are fewer managers and people have equal status
* *managing by consensus:* managing by getting everyone to agree

The Independent on Sunday

4 According to the text, which of these phrases are typically used by men and which by women?

Example:
'It's very simple. The point is ...'
Men because 'the male approach is to go to the heart of the matter'.

1 'But we need to take account of ...'

2 'You look worried. What do you think about the new plan?'

3 'That's rubbish!'

4 'I built the department from nothing.'

5 'Thanks for your kind words, but this really was a team effort.'

6 'It was so funny. He looked ridiculous!'

5 Work in groups and discuss the questions.

1 What is the style of male and female managers in companies in your country? Are they similar to the ones outlined in the text?

2 Do you think there is a difference in style between men and women or is any difference usually because of personality?

3 Do you know any men who have a 'female' style of working? or women who have a 'male' style of working?

4 Do you find it easier to work with men or women? Why?

6 Choose a spokesperson in the group to make a presentation to the whole class, summarising the opinions in the group.

Vocabulary

Word building

1 Complete the table with words from the text then mark the stress.

VERB	NOUN	ADJECTIVE
1 to compete (with)	competition	competitive
2 to confront	confrontation	_____
3 to collaborate	collaboration	_____
4 to control	_____	controlling
5 _____	encouragement	encouraging
6 to achieve	_____	achieving

2 Complete the following sentences using one of the words from the table.

1 It was a great _____ to win the company's prize for excellence.

2 This is a really difficult job at times. I'd like a bit of _____ from my boss occasionally.

3 I hate having meetings with Alan. He's always aggressive and _____.

4 I don't like working on my own, I need other people to _____ with.

5 It's impossible to _____ events, but you can influence them.

Writing   Clauses of contrast

1 Clauses of contrast give information which is surprising when compared to the main clause. Read the sentences and notice how the **conjunctions** introduce the clause of contrast.

1 Men and women have different styles **but** both can adopt the other gender's way of working.

2 **Although** the majority of employees in the company are women, men hold most of the senior management posts.

3 It is sometimes dangerous to generalise, **however** we can note some specific differences between men and women's styles.

Check your ideas with the Grammar Reference section.

2 Look at the chart comparing Chief Executive Officers' pay.

Work in pairs and write three sentences using clauses of contrast.

Examples:
Although all the pay is very high, it is higher in some countries than in others. Although basic pay for CEOs is similar in France and Italy, the total salary is higher in France.

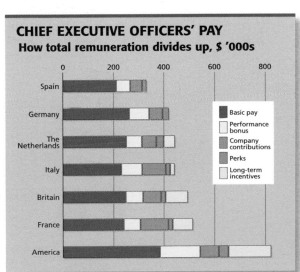

CHIEF EXECUTIVE OFFICERS' PAY
How total remuneration divides up, $ '000s

Basic pay
Performance bonus
Company contributions
Perks
Long-term incentives

► **Grammar Reference page 156**

Business Communication

Talking about your job

1 Work in pairs. Look at the cartoon and discuss what you think the job of a tour representative is like.

2 📻 8.6 Listen and complete the gaps.

Name: Lisa Crawford	
Job title: *Tour representative*	
Company she works for: ¹ _____ _____	
Perks: ² _____ _____	
Ratio of men to women: ³ _____	

3 📻 Listen again and complete the gaps.

Note the patterns:
responsible for +... ing
involves +...ing
deal with + noun

1 It involves _____.
2 I'm responsible for _____.
3 I have to deal with _____.
4 It also involves _____.

4 📻 Look at the list of jobs. Listen and identify which of these jobs the speaker describes.

 Customer Services Manager

 Shoe Designer

 Personnel Officer

 Shop Assistant

 Managing Director

 Advertising Executive

5 Work in pairs. Choose one of the other jobs and describe it to your partner. Your partner has to guess which job it is.

6 Think of a job; your own job, or one you would like in the future. Write a list of:

- the responsibilities
- the perks or extra benefits
- details such as the ratio of men and women colleagues

7 Work in pairs. Ask your partner about his/her job (from exercise 6). Use the language box to help you.

Finding out about someone's job	**Talking about your job**
What does your job involve?	I deal with _____
What do you do in your job?	I'm responsible for _____ ing
Do you have to ...?	I have to _____
	My job involves _____ ing

Final Task

Writing

Write your objectives and your action plan for getting a (new) job or promotion. Think about:

- skills you need to develop
- qualifications you need
- where you need to look for information and job advertisements

Checklist for Unit 8:

☐ 1 When we intend to do something in the future, what tense do we use?

☐ 2 When can we use the *will* future?

☐ 3 What is the negative contracted form of *will*?

☐ 4 What is the noun form of *to achieve*?

☐ 5 Make two sentences to compare male and female management styles.

In this unit:

- **Language Focus**
  Modal verbs: talking about possibility
  Present passive
  Pronunciation: word linking, stress patterns

- **Skills**
  Writing: connectors to show addition of information
  Reading: Marks & Spencer
  Listening: world competitive scoreboard

- **Vocabulary**
  Word building

- **Business Communication**
  Describing trends, interpreting graphs

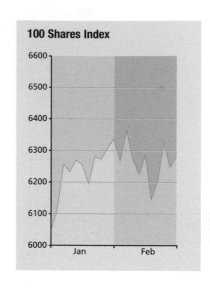

100 Shares Index

Key Vocabulary

🔲 **9.1** All businesses are affected by their immediate environment. Many factors influence them, for example, **availability of labour** (that is, how easy or difficult it is to find workers); **labour costs** (how much it costs to employ people) and **availability of raw materials**, such as oil and wood. The amount of money a company has to pay the government in **taxes** is another factor. Businesses are also affected by the **state of the economy.** In a period of **economic recession** many businesses suffer, their profits fall and they have to make **cuts**. In this climate there will be a rise in **unemployment**. These factors can affect sales and prices and change the **trend**, or direction, they move in.

Lead-in

1 Look at the shopping baskets which show the prices of everyday goods in five countries.

Answer the questions.

1 In which country is the shopping basket of everyday goods most expensive?
2 In which country is it least expensive?
3 What is the price difference between the most and least expensive countries?
4 What items do you think the shopping basket contains?
5 Why do you think the prices are different?

US

Japan

Switzerland

France

Canada

2 Read the text below to check your answer to exercise 1 question 5.

Many everyday brands which are used by people in almost every country can have varying prices throughout the world. Some of the variations in price are due to differences in exchange rates, some are due to the differences in local raw materials and production or shipping costs and some are due to variation in taxes.

However, the wide variation in prices for some brands cannot be explained by these factors and it may be that multi-national companies are charging what they think the market will bear.

Language Focus One

Modal verbs: talking about possibility

1 'The Big Mac Index' shows how long it takes in different countries to earn enough money to buy a Big Mac with French fries.

In Lagos it takes almost two full working days for the average worker to earn enough to buy a Big Mac and a large portion of French fries. In Tokyo it only takes 25 minutes.

1 How long must people work in Nairobi, Caracas, London and Budapest to buy a Big Mac and fries?

2 How much do a Big Mac and large fries cost in your country? How long do you have to work to buy them? (based on the average wage)

2 9.2 Listen to the following sentences. Do you think the speaker is sure about the reasons she gives for the price of Big Macs, or is she making educated guesses?

may, might

1 The average wage may be quite low in Caracas or a Big Mac might cost a lot there.

2 It takes a long time to earn enough to buy a Big Mac in Lagos. There may be a luxury tax on it in Nigeria.

can't, could

3 In Chicago the competition from other hamburger companies could affect the price.

4 I could be wrong, but I think the Big Mac and a portion of fries costs about £3.00 in London.

5 Big Macs may cost more to produce in Lagos, but it can't be because of the cost of labour. Labour costs are so low there.

Adverbs: *maybe, perhaps, probably*

6 Perhaps/Maybe Big Macs are more expensive in Britain because demand is high.

7 Salaries are probably higher in Frankfurt than in London.

NOTE: *maybe* is one word when it means *perhaps*. Compare the two sentences: *Maybe* demand is very high in Chicago. Demand in Chicago *may be* very high.

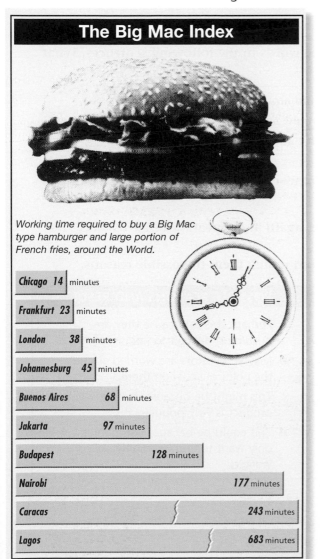

The Big Mac Index

Working time required to buy a Big Mac type hamburger and large portion of French fries, around the World.

Chicago **14**	minutes
Frankfurt **23**	minutes
London **38**	minutes
Johannesburg **45**	minutes
Buenos Aires **68**	minutes
Jakarta **97**	minutes
Budapest **128**	minutes
Nairobi **177**	minutes
Caracas **243**	minutes
Lagos **683**	minutes

3 True or false (T/F)?

> **1** We use *may*, *might*, *can* and *could* to talk about possibility.
> We don't use them if we are sure of something. T/F
>
> **2** *Can't* expresses stronger possibility than *could*. T/F

Form

The modal verbs *may*, *might*, *can't*, *could* are always followed by an **infinitive without to**:

Competition could affect the price.

▶ **Grammar Reference page 153**

Pronunciation One

Word linking

1 🔲 9.3a Listen to the following words. Can you hear the final letter?

> could   might   can't

2 🔲 9.3b Now listen to the same words in the following sentences. What do you notice about the final letter?

> **1** It **could** be true.   **4** It **could** arrive today.
> **2** You **might** be right.   **5** He **might** ask for an extra week.
> **3** That **can't** be right.   **6** It **can't** add up.

3 In each case, does the following word start with a vowel sound or a consonant sound?

4 🔲 9.3b Listen to the sentences again and repeat.

Language Practice One

1 Read the following sentences and match them to possible reasons.

FACTS	POSSIBLE REASONS AND RESULTS
1 There is high unemployment.	**a** Perhaps this is because they are becoming difficult to find.
2 No one wants to invest in the North.	**b** Maybe investors are worried about the political situation there.
3 A computer firm announces a massive profit.	**c** This might be because its new product is very popular.
4 The cost of raw materials will get higher.	**d** This could be because companies only want to employ highly skilled workers.

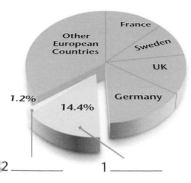

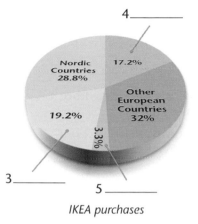

IKEA sales

IKEA purchases

2 📼 9.4 **Look at the two pie charts. Listen to a business analyst talking about IKEA. Add the names of countries and parts of the world to the charts.**

3 Work in pairs. **What are the possible reasons for the facts? Talk about IKEA's situation. Use the ideas in brackets to help you.**

1 Sales in Germany account for about 15% of the total.
   Example:
   This could be because the style of furniture is very popular in Germany.

2 Sales in Sweden account for a healthy 10% of total sales.
   (possible reasons: Swedish design of products, environmentally friendly, cost)

3 Sales in North America account for 14.4%.
   (possible reason: size of population)

4 19.2% of IKEA's purchases from suppliers come from the Far East.
   (possible reasons: low costs, availability of raw materials)

5 17.2% of purchases come from Eastern Europe.
   (possible reason: low labour costs)

6 Only 3.3% of purchases come from North America.
   (possible reason: high costs there)

Cross-cultural Comparison

Look at the chart which ranks countries according to competitiveness.

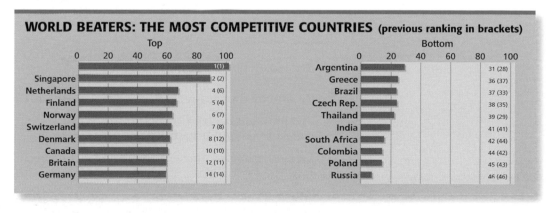

WORLD BEATERS: THE MOST COMPETITIVE COUNTRIES (previous ranking in brackets)

Top		Bottom	
	1 (1)	Argentina	31 (28)
Singapore	2 (2)	Greece	36 (37)
Netherlands	4 (6)	Brazil	37 (33)
Finland	5 (4)	Czech Rep.	38 (35)
Norway	6 (7)	Thailand	39 (29)
Switzerland	7 (8)	India	41 (41)
Denmark	8 (12)	South Africa	42 (44)
Canada	10 (10)	Colombia	44 (42)
Britain	12 (11)	Poland	45 (43)
Germany	14 (14)	Russia	46 (46)

Work in pairs. Choose three countries and discuss the reasons for their position on the scoreboard. Think about some of these points.

- political stability
- infrastructure
- inflation
- taxes
- labour costs
- international trade
- foreign investment
- technology

97

Listening

1 ▭ 9.5 Listen to Tom Armstrong talking about five countries on the scoreboard. Complete the table.

COUNTRY	POSITION	REASON
1 United States	Top/First	
2		
3		
4		
5		

2 Did Tom mention any of the three countries you discussed in the Cross-cultural comparison? Did you guess the reasons correctly?

Writing

Connectors to show addition of information

1 The words in bold are connectors that show the writer is adding more information. Read the examples to see how they are used.

1 The country is suffering for a number of reasons; the infrastructure is poor, there is little inward investment and workers are demotivated **too/as well**.

2 Like Finland, Norway **also** showed strong growth last year.

3 India benefits from low labour costs, and **in addition** raw materials are plentiful.

4 The Netherlands is in the top five countries. Finland is **as well**.

2 What do you notice about the position of the connectors? Match the connector with its position.

1	too/as well	**a**	end of clause
2	in addition	**b**	mid position
3	also	**c**	start of second clause or second sentence

3 Use one of the connectors to complete the following sentences.

1 Singapore has a very strong infrastructure. _____ there is a high level of trade and investment.

2 The Netherlands comes in the top five countries. Finland is _____ up in the top five.

3 High corporate taxes can have a negative effect on an economy. They reduce companies' profits and _____ they do not encourage foreign investment.

4 Although Poland is in 45th place, it shows a strong entrepreneurial spirit, and _____ it has a good rate of growth.

5 Britain is below Finand. Germany is _____ below Finland.

6 Ireland is now attracting a lot of foreign investment. Multinationals are opening offices there and more Irish people are staying in Ireland to work, _____.

4 Look at the information below. Choose one country and write a paragraph using connectors to show the addition of information.

country 1
- has very high inflation
- has high unemployment
- there is political instability
- has export difficulties
- President is in poor health

country 2
- low unemployment
- low corporate taxes
- a lot of foreign investment
- good growth
- skilled workforce

▶ **Grammar Reference page 157**

Language Focus Two

Present Passive

1 Look at the diagram of the car engine. The information around it shows where cars are made or developed. Which car manufacturers are featured, and what is the nationality of each?

ROVER   Nationality _____
Rover 200/400:
Developed with Honda of Japan, built in Oxford and Birmingham, UK.

NISSAN   Nationality _____
Primera, Micra, Primo Estate: Sunderland, UK
Almera Patrol, QX: Japan
Serena, Terano, Venet: Spain

VAUXHALL   Nationality _____
Astra: Ellesmere Port, UK; Eisenacht, Germany; Antwerp, Belgium
Classic Astra: Hungary and Poland
Corsa and Tigra: Zaragoza, Spain and Eisenacht, Germany
Sintra Engines: Ellesmere Port, UK. Built in Dorrevill, USA.
(Called Pontiac Adventure in USA, called Sintra in Europe.)

FIAT   Nationality _____
Seicento: Tychy, Poland

PEUGEOT   Nationality _____
206: Ryton near Coventry, UK. Over 50% of parts from UK. Other parts from EC countries.

2 Complete the sentences.
1 The Vauxhall Sintra is made in _____, _____.
2 The Nissan Primera is built in _____, UK.
3 The Fiat Seicento is made in _____, _____.
4 The Rover 200 is built at _____ and _____, UK.
5 The Peugeot 206 is built in _____, UK, and more than 50% of parts are sourced in the UK. The rest come from other EC countries.

3 **Look again at sentences 1 to 5 in exercise 2. They are in the passive form.**

1 Do we know who carries out the action in each sentence? (Who made the Vauxhall Sintra? Who built the Nissan Primera?)

2 Is it important to know who performs the action? (Are we interested in the factory workers in these sentences?)

3 Why does the writer use a passive sentence:
   'The Vauxhall Corsa is made in Zaragoza, Spain.'
   and not an active sentence:
   'Spanish workers make the Vauxhall Corsa'?

4 **Complete the sentences.**

1 We form a passive with the correct part of the verb _____ + the past _____.

2 The o_____ of an active verb becomes the s_____ of a passive verb.

   Active: Spanish workers make (Vauxhall cars.)
   OBJECT
   Passive: (Vauxhall cars) are made in Zaragoza.
   SUBJECT

3 In _____ sentences you do not need to include the 'doer', i.e. the person or thing which performs the action, because this is not an important piece of information.

Now check your answers in the Grammar reference.

► **Grammar Reference page 154**

Language Practice Two

1 **Write the following paragraph using the passive form of the verb in brackets. Be careful with the past participles.**

The Vauxhall Sintra

The engines [1] (manufacture) at Ellesmere Port in the UK. The cars [2] (build) in the US and [3] (sell) there as the Pontiac. Cars [4] (ship) back to the UK and [5] (sell) as the Sintra.

2 The business environment is becoming more technologically advanced. Look at the diagram which shows how interactive telephone services work.

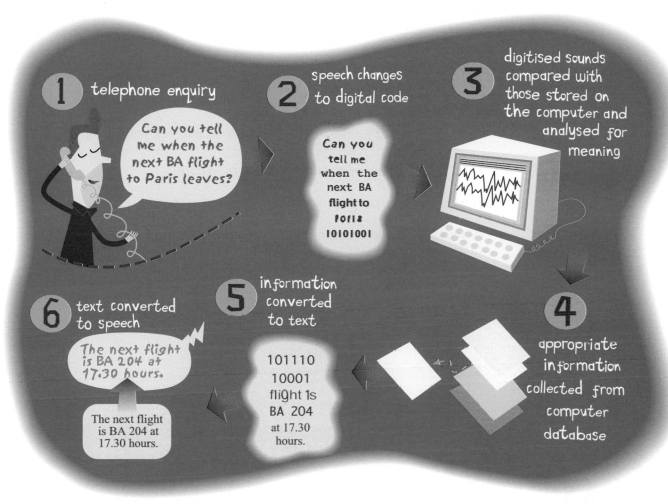

Independent on Sunday

3 In the six sentences which describe the illustrations above, the writer uses *telegraphic language* to keep the sentences short. Complete the six sentences in full.

Example:
1 *A telephone enquiry is made.*

1 A telephone enquiry _____ _____ .

2 The speech _____ _____ to digital code.

3 The digitised sounds _____ _____ with those on the computer and _____ _____ for meaning.

4 The appropriate information _____ _____ from the computer database.

5 The information _____ _____ to text.

6 The text _____ _____ to speech.

4 Work in pairs. Describe a process you are familiar with to your partner.

Reading

1 The newspaper article below is about Marks & Spencer (M&S). Read the first paragraph. What were profits like when the text was written?

2 Read paragraph 2 and say which two sectors Marks & Spencer deals in. Which one is doing well?

3 On the retailing side M&S is involved in various product ranges. Read paragraphs 3–5 and say which of the following are mentioned.

1 home furnishings	**2** jewellery	**3** food
4 clothing and footwear	**5** newspapers and magazines	**6** sports goods

Which area of business is M&S going to expand?

4 Which three markets do paragraphs 6, 7 and 8 describe?

5 Read the topic sentences in paragraphs 6, 7 and 8. Are profits up or down in all three markets?

6 Which word describes the trend for each market? Match a phrase with the correct market.

Markets   **Trends**

1 Far East   **a** profits were hit
2 Europe   **b** profits fell
3 North America   **c** suffered a downturn

7 Which factor in the business environment affected sales in each market?

NO QUICK RESPITE IN SIGHT FOR M&S*

1 **MARKS & SPENCER** suffered at home and abroad during the first half of its financial year and the company admits that trading in recent weeks has shown no signs of improvement.

2 The group makes the vast majority of its profits in Britain and these fell 20.2% to £316.5 million in the six months to 26 September. The figures were slightly boosted* by a good performance from financial services, where profits rose 19% to £44.9 million. Retailing profits fell almost £88 million to £271.9 million.

3 Sales of home furnishings showed the biggest decline, with a fall of 1.6% over the half year and 7.1% in the second quarter. Clothing and footwear sales were 2.3% ahead in the six month period but fell 0.3% in the last three months from a 4.9% increase in the first quarter.

4 Food was the most resilient area: it rose 2.1% overall, and maintained positive sales growth over the entire six-month period.

5 M&S is focusing on a range of initiatives in its food departments, including butcher shops, delicatessen counters*, bakeries and coffee shops. These are expected to be introduced into 100 stores as quickly as possible.

6 Overseas, the Far East suffered the worst downturn, reflecting continuing economic trouble in the region. The group made a £1.2 million loss overseas, compared with £10.8 million profit in 1997.

7 Europe was also hit, primarily by the impact of the strong pound.

8 North American profits also fell from £2 million to £1.2 million.

* *No Quick Respite in Sight for M&S*: there is no sign that business will improve rapidly for M&S
* *boosted*: improved
* *delicatessen counter*: a section of a shop which sells special cheeses, cooked meat, salads etc.

Evening Standard

Vocabulary

Word building

1 The text describes the trends for M&S's profits in key markets. Put each word from the box in the table.

1	improvement *(n)* (para 1)	4	decline *(n)* (para 3)
2	fell *(v)* (para 2)	5	increase *(n)* (para 3)
3	rose *(v)* (para 2)	6	maintained *(v)* (para 4)

rising

no change

falling

VERBS	NOUNS	VERBS	NOUNS	VERBS	NOUNS
to improve	*an improvement*	to _____		to _____	a _____
to _____	a _____	to _____		to _____	a _____
to _____	an _____			to _____	a _____
to _____				to _____	a _____

2 Now add the following words to the table.

a fall	a rise	a decrease	a drop
to increase	to grow	to decline	
to decrease	to drop	to stabilise	

Pronunciation Two

Stress patterns

1 9.6a Listen to how the verb and noun are pronounced. Repeat.

verb	noun
to incréase	an íncrease
to decréase	a décrease
to impórt	an ímport
to expórt	an éxport

2 9.6b Listen to seven sentences. Do you hear the noun or the verb?

**Business
Communication**

Describing trends

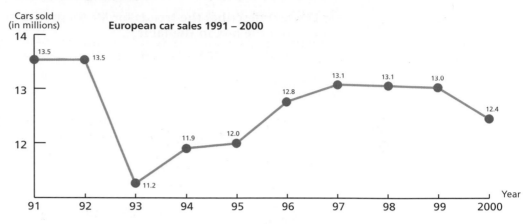

Cars sold (in millions)

European car sales 1991 – 2000

13.5 13.5 11.2 11.9 12.0 12.8 13.1 13.1 13.0 12.4

14 — 13 — 12 —

Year

91 92 93 94 95 96 97 98 99 2000

1 The graph shows car sales from 1991 to 2000.
Look at the graph and read these sentences.

> **Notice how the verbs + prepositions are used.**
> * **From** 1992 **to** 1993 car registrations **decreased from** 13.5 million **to** 11.2 million.
> * Car registrations **increased from** 11.2 million in 1993 **to** 11.9 million in 1994.
> * They **decreased by** about three hundred thousand (300,000) from 1991 to 1997.
> * There was **a decrease of** about half a million from 1991 to 1996.

Now complete these sentences using the graph.

1 ᵃ_____ 1993 ᵇ_____ 1994 registrations rose ᶜ_____ about 7,000 (seven thousand).

2 There was a decrease _____ about 2.3 (two point three) million from 1992 to 1993.

3 Car registrations rose ᵃ_____ about 11.2 (eleven point two) million in 1993 ᵇ_____ about 12.8 (twelve point eight) million in 1996.

2 Look at the graph again. When was:

1 the biggest decrease?   3 the smallest increase?

2 the biggest increase?   4 the smallest decrease?

> We can use **verb + adverb** to describe a trend.
> **Verb + adverb**
> Car sales *fell dramatically* from 1992 to 1993.
> They *rose steadily* from 1993 to 1997.
> They *dropped slightly* from 1997 to 1999.
> Sales *increased considerably*.
> Sales *fell sharply* from 1999 to 2000.

3 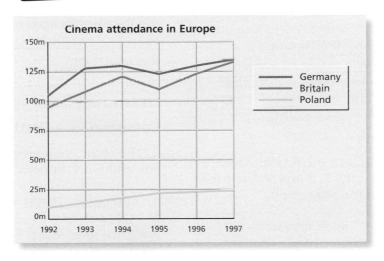 9.7 Listen to the sentences describing the graph on page 104. Are the sentences true or false?

4 Work in pairs. Choose a year from the graph and describe it. Your partner has to guess which year it is.

▶ **Grammar Reference page 159**

Final Task

1 Work in pairs. **Student A**: Read the rolecard below.
　　　　　　　　　Student B: Read the rolecard on page 148.

STUDENT A

Look at the graph below which shows cinema attendance for Poland, Germany and Britain.

* Describe the trend to your partner.
* Ask him/her about attendance in France and Italy.

Complete the graph.

Cinema attendance in Europe

Germany
Britain
Poland

150m
125m
100m
75m
50m
25m
0m

1992　1993　1994　1995　1996　1997

2 Discuss the possible reasons for the trend.

* free time
* ticket price
* quality of films
* advertising
* how much money people have
* number of different films

3 Write a short report about cinema-going in Europe.

▶ **Business Writing Workbook page 69**

Checklist for Unit 9:

☐ **1** Why are goods more expensive in some countries than in others?

☐ **2** What verbs can we use to give possible reasons?

☐ **3** When do we use the passive?

☐ **4** Think of three verbs to describe a downward ↘ trend.

☐ **5** Think of three verbs to describe an upward ↗ trend.

Products, People and the Business Environment

Business Review

The Internet offers a real opportunity for retailers and service providers to advertise their goods and services. Banking is a growth area, and many banks now offer Internet banking services. Most Net users are married males in their 30s. Security is the number one concern for users, and they are asked to register a security code each time they access their account.

1 Which service is becoming popular? What do you think the USPs and the benefits of the service are?

2 What problem exists in the IT business environment?

3 Is it clear who asks customers to register their security code? Why/Why not?

Vocabulary Review

All the words and phrases in the box are from the Key Vocabulary in units 7, 8 and 9. Use each word once to complete the paragraph.

raw materials	salary	social interaction
labour	customer profile	status	features
labour costs	benefits	advertisement
taxes	styles of management

A company's marketing department should decide what type of person will buy their product and have a ^{1}_____ _____ or description of the consumer in mind. Then they can design their advertisements. A good ^{2}_____ should describe the ^{3}_____ or characteristics of the product as well as the ^{4}_____ or advantages of buying the product.
The price of a product depends on various factors. Production costs are affected by the availability of ^{5}_____, or workers and the availability of ^{6}_____, or the things needed to make the goods. How much the company has to pay the workers, or ^{7}_____, is another factor, and also the amount the government charges the company in ^{8}_____.
The people who work for a company, or the company's labour force are the company's most important asset. Many different things motivate people to work, such as ^{9}_____ , or money, ^{10}_____ or the position they have in the company and society and the opportunity for ^{11}_____ _____ and to meet other people. Different people like different things, and the way managers treat employees, i.e. their ^{12}_____ _____ _____ can be very important.

Grammar Review

Comparative adjectives

1 The chart compares three hairdryers. Choose one and work in pairs to answer the questions.

REMINGTON 'TRAVEL PLUS' HAIRDRYER
- 1200 watt
- 2 heat/speed settings
- 120/230V ac
- travel size
- £7.75

PHILIPS HP4362 'ACTIVE' HAIRDRYER
- 1650 watt
- 6 combinations of heat/speed including 2 cool settings
- 230V ac only
- standard size
- £13.99

VIDAL SASSOON VS 722 HAIRDRYER
- 1800 watt
- 3 heat settings, 2 speed settings
- 230V ac only
- standard size
- £16.75

FEATURES	BENEFITS
1 How powerful is it?	*It will get hot more quickly.*
2 How many settings does it have?	
3 What is the voltage?	
4 How big is it?	
5 How much does it cost?	

2 What are the benefits to the customer of each feature? Complete the table.

3 Write five sentences describing the features and benefits of the hairdryers.

> e.g. *The Philips 'Active' is more powerful than the Remington 'Travel Plus', which means that when I use it it will get hot quickly.*

Order of adjectives, modal verbs of probability

1 Choose four objects that you can see. For each one write three words that describe it.

2 Put the adjectives in the right order.

3 Work in pairs. Student A: Give your partner the three adjectives. Student B: Use modal verbs of probability to guess the noun.

> Example A: *it's small, Japanese, and plastic.*
> B: *It could be a calculator.*

Going to for future

Think about your plans for later this year, next year, and for the next 2–3 years. Ask and answer questions in pairs about each other's plans.

Present passive

What is the main focus of these two sentences? *Coke* or the *people*?

1 The word *coke* is used to describe any type of cola drink.

2 Many people use the word *coke* to describe any type of cola drink.

Business Communication Review

1 Think of a product you bought some time this year. Write down:

- four adjectives to describe it
- its features
- its benefits

Prepare a one minute presentation to persuade your listener(s) to buy one.

2 Mark each of the verbs and nouns with an arrow (↗↘→) to show the trend it describes:

> **Verbs:** to improve   to decline   to rise
> to increase   to decrease   to stabilise
> to fall   to grow   to maintain (position)
> to drop

> **Nouns:** a fall   a drop   a rise   an increase
> a decline   a decrease

3 Look at the graph. Write a paragraph to describe it using the verbs and nouns in exercise 2.

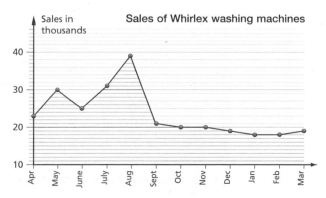

10 *Finance*

In this unit:

- **Language Focus**
  Figures and numbers
  Transitive and intransitive verbs
  Pronunciation: saying numerals,
  word recognition

- **Skills**
  Writing: rephrasing and exemplifying
  Reading: investment bank accounts
  Listening: profit and loss accounts

- **Vocabulary**
  Word partners

- **Business Communication**
  Scale of probability

Key Vocabulary

⬚ **10.1** Companies and individuals often **borrow** money, and it is important to find a favourable **interest rate**. Rates are variable, and can **rise** or **fall** depending on the market. Many **investors**, (people who use their money to earn more money), choose foreign or **offshore bank accounts** because they are tax-free. Anyone can buy shares in a **public company** and become a **shareholder**. All public companies in the UK are obliged by law to publish their **financial results** at the end of the **tax year**. They do this in their **annual report** to shareholders. Annual reports include **profit and loss accounts** which show **turnover**, or the total sum of money which is coming into the company.

Lead-in Work in pairs and answer the quiz questions.

How Much do you Know About Money?

1 Why do public companies publish annual reports?

2 Who uses the information in a profit and loss account?

3 A balance sheet shows total assets and total liabilities: Which term refers to what the company owns and which refers to the company's debts?

4 Do the directors or the shareholders own the company?

5 A dividend is the share of the _____ that the shareholders receive.

6 Which word means the total sum of money which is coming into the company?

7 Profit minus the costs associated with preparing the goods for sale is called gross/net profit.

8 The total profit without subtracting costs and overheads is called gross/net profit.

Language Focus One

Figures and numbers

1 Look at the five lists of numbers and choose a term from the box that describes each one.

cardinal numbers	fractions	decimal numbers
ordinal numbers	percentages	

1 _____   0   15   30   45 ....

2 _____   1st   2nd   3rd ....

3 _____ $1/4$ $1/2$ $3/4$ 1 $1/3$ $2/3$ ....

4 _____   0.25   0.50   0.75 ....

5 _____   9%   18% .... 36% ....

2 Add the next number(s) to each sequence and then say them.

Pronunciation

Saying numerals

1 Look at the written form of the dates, times, money and dimensions. Can you say them?

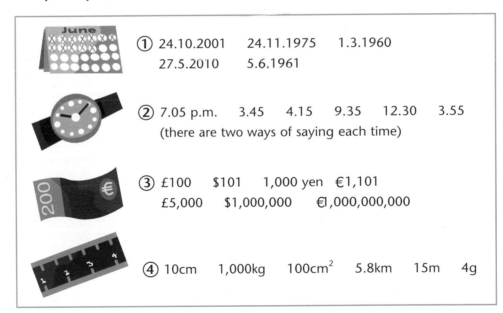

① 24.10.2001   24.11.1975   1.3.1960
27.5.2010   5.6.1961

② 7.05 p.m.   3.45   4.15   9.35   12.30   3.55
(there are two ways of saying each time)

③ £100 $101   1,000 yen   €1,101
£5,000 $1,000,000   €1,000,000,000

④ 10cm   1,000kg   100cm^2 5.8km   15m   4g

▭ 10.2 Listen and repeat the numerals.

2 Work in pairs. Student A reads the numerals to Student B. Student B listens to the numerals and writes them down without looking at this page.

a $100,000	b 29.12.2004	c 11.20p.m.	d 7.9 km
e $99	f 17.6.2003	g 5.45	h 10.45

Check your answers.

3 Change roles. Student B reads the list on page 148 to Student A.

► **Grammar Reference page 160**

Language Practice One

Cardinal numbers

1 A minimum wage was finally set in Britain in 1999. Workers were very happy, but employers were not. Why is this?

2 📼 10.3 Listen and complete the paragraph.

> In 1999 the minimum wage was set at [1] £ _____ for adults and [2] £ _____ for young workers aged between eighteen and twenty-one. Employers wanted the minimum wage to be [3] £ _____ but workers wanted it set at [4] £ _____.

3 Is there a minimum wage in your country? Do you think governments should set a minimum wage?

Ordinal numbers

1 Look at the chart on the left. It shows the world ranking of the cost of living in 13 European cities.

2 📼 10.4 Listen and complete the gaps in the chart.

THE MOST EXPENSIVE CITIES IN THE WORLD

	This year	Last year
a	5	3
Zurich	6	3
b	7	6
Geneva	8	5
c	10	28
Stockholm	13	8
Copenhagen	14	8
Vienna	14	8
Dusseldorf	d	14
Lyon	e	15
Amsterdam	24	21
Helsinki	24	23
f	26	26

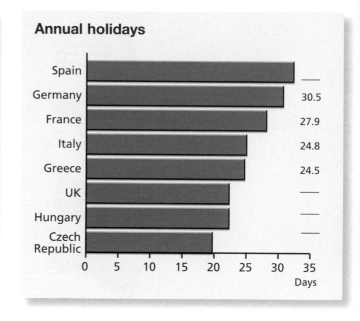

Annual holidays

Spain _____
Germany 30.5
France 27.9
Italy 24.8
Greece 24.5
UK _____
Hungary _____
Czech Republic _____

Days

Decimals

1 Look at the bar chart on the right showing annual holidays in eight different countries.

2 📼 10.5 Listen and complete the figures at the end of each bar.

Percentages

1 **Look at the pie chart which shows the average weekly expenditure of a British person. Work in pairs and answer the questions.**

What percentage of their weekly budget does the average Briton spend on:

1 housing, transport, household goods and services?

2 leisure goods and services, tobacco?

3 food and drink, clothing and footwear?

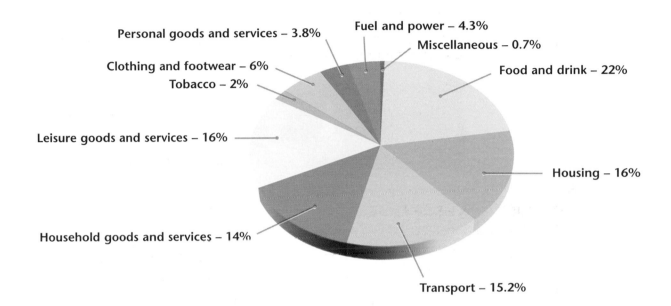

Personal goods and services – 3.8%
Fuel and power – 4.3%
Miscellaneous – 0.7%
Clothing and footwear – 6%
Food and drink – 22%
Tobacco – 2%
Leisure goods and services – 16%
Housing – 16%
Household goods and services – 14%
Transport – 15.2%

Source: *Family Spending, Stationery Office*

2 **For each of the categories make a list of typical items they include. Say if expenditure is essential or non-essential.**

Example: **Transport:** *train fares to work, petrol – essential*

3 ▭ 10.6 **Listen to two people discussing their weekly expenditure and complete the table.**

	Matthew (male)	Robyn (female)	Pie chart
Food and drink			22%
Housing		Not given	16%
Transport			15.2%
Household goods and services			14%
Leisure goods and services			16%
Tobacco		0%	2%

4 Make your own pie chart showing your weekly expenditure.

5 Work in pairs. Tell each other how the percentages in the table compare with yours.

Reading

1 The text is about an offshore investment account with Jyske Bank. Why do people choose offshore accounts?

Treat yourself to a euro deposit

1 If you want to send your money offshore, you need the best account available, with the flexibility to meet your investment goals. You need our No. 1 Account. So why not give yourself a present – send your money offshore and let Jyske Bank help you take care of it.

2 **Benefits that can't be beaten**
Why do we say our accounts are more flexible? Well, for a start you'll get an on-demand, interest-bearing account offered in more than 25 different currencies. Plus, you can switch between currencies free of charge to take full advantage of interest and exchange-rate benefits, regardless of the currency of your deposit. You can even have a VISA card.

3 **No. 1 – in more than one sense**
The No. 1 Account offers so many advantages that it is the only

proper name for it. But we are also No. 1 in other areas. Our professional account managers are well-informed as to current market developments, and would be pleased to draw up a proposal which matches your requirements.

4 **Personal, quality service**
You can open an account in Gibraltar or Copenhagen and you'll always receive a high level of friendly, personal service. That's our promise. To receive the maximum benefit from the investment opportunities, we recommend a deposit of minimum £10,000.

5 **Interested?**
Don't wait a minute longer to begin reaching your investment goals. Contact Jyske Bank today for further information about our No. 1 Account and other opportunities.

London Branch	**Telephone:**	0171 264 7700
Address: FREEPOST LON,	**Fax:**	0171 264 7717
10/12 Alie Street	**E-mail:**	jyskebank@jyskebank.co.uk
London E1 8BR	**Internet:**	www.jyske-bank.dk/pb

JYSKE BANK

2 Read the introduction *(paragraph 1)*. What is the name of the account that Jyske Bank is offering?

3 Read paragraphs 2–5 quickly, then match them to these summary sentences.

a Our customer care is excellent.   paragraph ☐

b Our staff are top finance people.   paragraph ☐

c What you should do next.   paragraph ☐

d The account is flexible and offers several benefits. paragraph ☐

Writing

Rephrasing and exemplifying

1 Read this summary of the text and notice how the **connectors** are used.

The proposition
Send your money offshore and put it in our flexible No. 1 Account. We will help you take care of it.

The Benefits
Our accounts are very flexible. **For example**, you can open an interest-bearing account in more than 25 currencies. There are other benefits too; you can switch between currencies free of charge, and you can have a VISA card.

The leading bank account
The account has so many advantages that No. 1 is the only proper name for it, **in other words** it is really a leader. We are also leaders in other areas, **such as** account management. Our account managers are well-informed about the market and can draw up proposals for you.

The service
It is possible to open an account in two countries; Copenhagen or Gibraltar. **That means** you can choose the location that suits you. We'll always offer you a friendly service. We recommend a minimum deposit to get the maximum benefits from the account, **i.e.** £10,000.

The next step
Contact Jyske Bank now for further information.

---

2 Which connectors in the box below show that two pieces of information are the same and which ones present an example?

in other words	that is to say (i.e.)	that means
such as	for example (e.g.)	

3 Choose a connector to complete the gaps.

1 There are several advantages to offshore banking, *for example* you don't have to pay tax.

2 There are a number of different accounts, _____ a high interest account, or an instant access account.

3 All investment carries some risk _____ your investment may go down as well as up.

4 It's important to make sure that you get a good return on your investment _____ that you make money.

5 Interest rates don't always rise, they may fall, _____ they are variable.

6 All businesses have assets _____ buildings, land, machinery, investments, cash, stock, etc.

4 Match the expressions below. Then join them with a connecting word or phrase.

Example:
The interest rate is 2% above the bank base rate. **In other words** *it's 7%.*

1 To benefit from the higher rate of interest you need to have $1000 in your account.	a It's 7%.
	b You have to pay more for the money you borrow than you will receive for the money you save.
2 The interest rate is 2% above the bank rate.	
3 Many banks have an international presence.	c You get a lower rate of interest with less than $1000.
4 The rate of interest for borrowing is always higher than for saving.	d Deutsche Bank, Parisbas Sumitomo, and NatWest.

➤ **Grammar Reference page 157**

Vocabulary

Word partners

1 Read the two sentences. Which words are used as partners to the noun *account*?

Jyske Bank is offering an *offshore* **account**.
Its No. 1 Account is an *interest-bearing* **account**.

Account **can also have other partners:**   *bank* account
                                             current account
                                             deposit account

2 Write a list of other adjectives that are partners to the noun *manager*.
Example: *personnel* manager.

3 **The noun and the definition are matched. Choose the correct adjective to complete the word partners.**

Example: *1f*

ADJECTIVE	NOUN	DEFINITION
1 annual	a opportunity	= A chance to make your money work for you.
2 interest	b chart	= A circular graph divided into sectors.
3 investment	c sheet	= A document showing assets and liabilities.
4 operating	d number	= A number which shows order or sequence.
5 balance	e number	= A number which shows quantity.
6 net	f report	= A yearly publication showing a company's financial position.
7 ordinal	g cost	= How much companies spend on workers' wages.
8 cardinal	h profit	= How much the company is making after deducting production costs.
9 labour	i rate	= The amount the bank charges you to borrow money.
10 pie	j profit	= The gross profits minus the cost of overheads.

Language Focus Two

Transitive and intransitive verbs: *rise, raise, arise*

1 **These three verbs are often confused. Look at the three pairs of sentences and for each one say if the verb is followed by a direct object (*a transitive verb*) or not (*an intransitive verb*).**

Rise	*Each year Interest rates rise.* *Last year Interest rates rose.*	Is there a direct object?
Raise	*We'll raise our prices by 2% in April.* *The bank raised our overdraft.*	Is there a direct object?
Arise	*I hope this situation will not arise again.* *The problem arose because the machine wasn't working properly.*	Is there a direct object?

2 **Which verb has a regular past tense and which verbs have an irregular past tense?**

3 **Match each verb with the correct meaning.**

1 Raise   a to increase, go up or reach a higher level

2 Arise   b to put up or make higher

3 Rise   c to occur, appear or become evident

4 Complete the table.

	TRANSITIVE/INTRANSITIVE	SIMPLE PAST	PAST PARTICIPLE
rise			risen
raise			raised
arise			arisen

▶ **Grammar Reference page 154**

Pronunciation

Word recognition

1 🔲 10.7a Listen and number the words in the order you hear them.

a rise ☐   b raise ☐   c arise ☐
d rose ☐   e raised ☐   f arose ☐

2 🔲 10.7b Listen and repeat the words.

3 🔲 10.7c Listen and repeat the sentences in Language Focus Two, exercise 1.

Language Practice Two

1 Select the correct sentence from each group.

1 a Interest rates raised by 1%.
  b The bank might raise the interest rate.
  c The interest rate will raise.

2 a A problem arose with the account.
  b It arose a problem.
  c It will not arise this problem again.

3 a The bank will rise the prices soon.
  b Prices rose by 3% last year.
  c Our supplier rose their prices last year.

4 a The bank is going to raise our credit level.
  b Their prices raised in April.
  c The prices might raise.

5 a It arises a problem.
  b He arised a problem at the meeting.
  c The same problem might arise on the new account.

6 a This rises a problem.
  b The rate of inflation is rising steadily.
  c The bank will rise the overdraft.

2 Choose the correct verb and tense to complete the sentences.

1 The company's turnover _____ dramatically last year.

2 That's a good point, I'll _____ it at the next sales meeting.

3 Several difficulties _____ when we tried to install the new software.

4 Interest rates _____ last year.

5 The government _____ interest rates last month.

6 I hope the problem of late payment will not _____ again.

Listening

1 Look at the profit and loss account for a telecommunications company.

Consolidated profit and loss account

	2000 £m	1999 £m
Turnover		
Continuing operations	1,642.4	1,402.2
Acquisition	106.6	-
	1,749.0	1,402.2
Operating profit		
Continuing operations	521.3	465.8
Acquisitions	8.3	-
	529.6	465.8
Disposal of fixed asset investment	25.9	7.2
Profit on ordinary activities before interest	555.5	473.0
Net interest (payable)/receivable	16.4	2.1
Profit on ordinary activities before Taxation	539.1	475.1
Tax on profit on ordinary activities	171.9	164.6
Profit on ordinary activities after taxation	367.2	310.5
Equity minority interests	3.4	0.7
Profit for the financial year	363.8	309.8
Equity dividends	147.5	122.6
Retained profit for the financial year	216.3	187.2
Earnings per share	11.89p	10.15p

2 Before you listen tell your partner what you know about:

1 what a 'profit and loss account' is

2 why managers are interested in it

3 why shareholders are interested in it

4 *turnover, operating profit, earnings per share*

3 🔲 **10.8 Listen and complete the summary. Check your information.**

The Profit and Loss Account

A profit and loss account is [1] _____ .

The information in a profit and loss account helps managers [2] _____ .

A profit and loss account tells shareholders [3] _____ .

Information for Managers

Turnover shows managers [4] _____ and if the company is
[5] _____ .

Operating profit shows [6] _____ .

This tells managers [7] _____ .

Information for Shareholders

Earnings per share shows shareholders [8] _____ . In this case
[9] _____

Cross-cultural Comparison

Work in pairs and discuss.

1 Are companies in your country required to publish their financial results? Do you think this is good practice or not?

2 Do you own any shares in a company? Which companies in your country offer a safe investment to shareholders?

3 Are interest rates high or low in your country? Is this good for investors? Is it good for the economy?

4 Who sets interest rates in your country? Government or the Central Bank?

5 Many British pop stars move to other countries to avoid paying high taxes. or they put their money in offshore accounts. Which country nearest to yours offers tax-free, offshore accounts? Do you think offshore accounts are a good idea? Why/Why not?

Business Communication

Scale of probability

1 When we make financial predictions, we can feel sure or unsure about them. Look at the scale of probability which shows different levels of certainty.

100%	Certainty	I'm sure/certain that share prices will (definitely) rise.
75%	Probability	{ It's likely that share prices will increase. Share prices should increase.
50%	Possibility	Share prices may/might increase.
25%	Improbability	{ It's (very) unlikely that share prices will increase. Share prices are unlikely to increase.
0%	Impossibility	I'm sure/certain that share prices (definitely) won't increase.

Work in pairs. **Student A:** Use the language in the box to ask Student B about the future of:

1 share prices   2 the cost of living   3 interest rates
4 profits for a major company in your country

> Are you sure that ... will ...?
>
> Do you think ... might ...?
>
> Are you sure that ... won't ...?

Student B: Give answers to Student A's questions.

> Example: **A:** *'Are you sure that share prices of Coca-Cola will rise this year?'*
>   **B:** *'Yes, I'm certain that they'll rise this year.'*

2 Change partners and practise asking and answering again.

3 Work in pairs. **Student A:** read the notes on page 149.
               Student B: Read the notes on page 147.

➤ **Grammar Reference page 153**

Final Task

Cadbury Schweppes to sell its drinks business

CADBURY Schweppes is selling off all its drinks business, apart from its brands in the US.
Its share price increased by nearly 6% to 988p, an increase of 541.5 p. It is selling its soft drinks brands to Coca-Cola for $1.85 billion.

Work in pairs and discuss.

1 Why do you think Cadbury is selling its soft drinks? How will this make the company stronger?

2 When they announced the news, do you think people wanted to buy shares? Why? What effect did this have on the share price?

3 Why do you think Coca-Cola wanted to buy the brands? How will this make the company stronger?

4 Do you think the sale price is good?

Checklist for Unit 10:

☐ 1 Say these numerals. €5,000 $7 1.5 million 7.35 10cm 55%

☐ 2 What are the advantages of an account with Jyske Bank?

☐ 3 What does a profit and loss account show?

☐ 4 Make three sentences with these verbs: *raise rise arise*

☐ 5 What do you think will happen to inflation in your country in the next six months?

In this unit:

- **Language Focus**
  Conditional 1: events and consequences
  Gerunds and infinitives
  Pronunciation: short forms

- **Skills**
  Writing: *both ... and, either ... or, neither ... nor*
  Reading: late payment of commercial debts
  Listening: the ethical consumer

- **Vocabulary**
  Word groups

- **Business Communication**
  Negotiating

Key Vocabulary

🔲 11.1 Market research shows that many consumers are '**ethical consumers**'; they expect the companies they buy from to behave responsibly. Most ethical consumers have high **spending power** so companies usually listen to them and will promise, for example, not to use child labour or to pollute the **environment**. A recent report showed that many companies have an **ethical policy** which covers areas such as **payment on time, product policy** and the environment. Some companies have a policy of paying '**first world**' prices for '**third world**' goods from developing countries – they pay more because they think the workers and the economies of developing countries need support.

Lead-in

1 **Which of these responsibilities do you think a company should have?**

Responsibilities

1 There should be good communication between the company and its workforce.

2 The company should pay suppliers on time.

3 The company should have an equal opportunities policy; in other words, people of all races and both sexes should be equal.

4 It should train its employees.

5 It should try to protect and improve the environment.

6 It should make a profit so it can pay dividends to its shareholders and continue to provide jobs for its workforce.

7 It should help with the local education of young people.

8 It should be active in the local community.

KEY
3 = very important
2 = quite important
1 = not important

2 Match the responsibilities with the benefit.

Benefits to company

a It will attract loyal employees.

b It will attract loyal customers.

c It will improve the quality of its workforce.

d It will help improve national economic health.

e It will benefit from long-term gains.

f It will benefit from good business partnerships.

g People will want to invest in the company.

Language Focus one

Conditional 1: events and consequences

1 A consultant advises CleanHome, a detergent manufacturer.

'If you don't behave responsibly towards the environment...   ethical consumers will stop buying your products.'

('If' clause) ⟷ (main clause)

'Your profits will fall...   if consumers stop buying your products '

(main clause) ⟷ ('If' clause)

2 📼 11.2 Listen to the rest of the discussion and fill the gaps.

CH = CleanHome Manager   MC = Management Consultant

CH: What'll happen _____ our profits fall?

MC: _____ your profits fall the shareholders' dividend _____ decrease.

CH: If our shareholders' dividend decreases they'll be very unhappy.

MC: Yes, your situation _____ very serious if the public loses confidence in the company.

CH: Our share price might fall if people _____ confidence. I think we should consider this matter seriously.

3 Circle an answer to give the Conditional 1 grammar rules.

1 Conditional 1 sentences are made up of 1 /② clauses.

2 The main clause describes **a situation or event/consequence**.

3 The *if* clause describes **a situation or event/consequence**.

4 It is **important/not important** which clause comes first.

5 In the main clause use *will/if* + infinitive.

6 In the *if* clause use *if* + **present tense/*will***.

7 We **can/cannot** use *might* instead of *will* if we are not sure about the consequence.

8 Short forms of *will* and *will not* are **often/never** used in spoken conditionals.

Language Practice One

1 Complete the sentences with the correct tenses.

Example:
*If a company **conducts** irresponsible marketing, customers **will not buy** its products.*

1 If a company (to conduct) irresponsible marketing, customers (not buy) its products.

2 A small company (to go out of business) if its customers (not pay) on time.

3 Many customers (not buy) products if companies (to test) them on animals.

4 If a multinational company (to pay) 'first world' prices for goods from developing countries, the suppliers (to become) self-sufficient.

5 If a company (to delay) payments, what (to be) the consequences?

▶ **Grammar Reference page 152**

Pronunciation

Short form of *will/will not*

2 🔲 11.3 Listen to the sentences then repeat.

1 How are *will/will not* pronounced in Conditional 1 sentences?

2 How is *will* pronounced in the question form?

3 Match the Cooperative bank's policy statements with the photos.

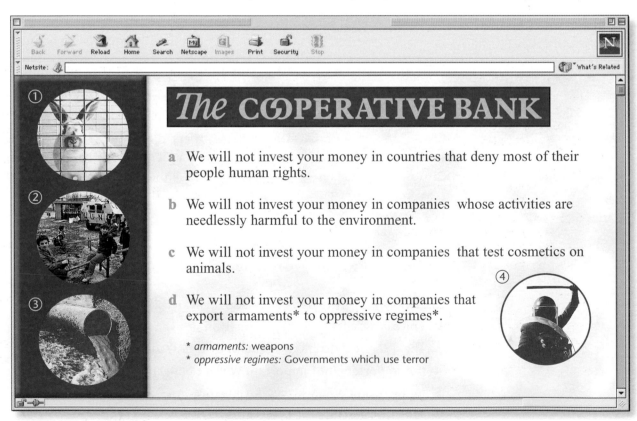

The COOPERATIVE BANK

a We will not invest your money in countries that deny most of their people human rights.

b We will not invest your money in companies whose activities are needlessly harmful to the environment.

c We will not invest your money in companies that test cosmetics on animals.

d We will not invest your money in companies that export armaments* to oppressive regimes*.

* *armaments*: weapons
* *oppressive regimes*: Governments which use terror

Cooperative Bank website

4 Write a conditional 1 sentence for each extract a–d.

Example: 1a *If a country denies its people their human rights, the Cooperative Bank will not invest your money in it.*

Reading

1 In the UK, where late payment is frequent, the government is considering a new law. Read paragraph one and complete this sentence.

If a larger business ¹_____ _____ , a smaller business ²_____ _____ _____ to charge interest on the debt.

2 Read paragraph three and complete the graph to show the average payment times of Finnish, Danish, Swedish, German and UK companies. (Don't include the information from the NatWest survey.)

Name, shame and claim from late payers*

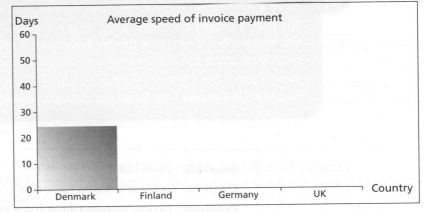

1 The Late Payment of Commercial Debts Bill* will soon become law. When it does, small businesses which employ fewer than 50 people will have the right to charge a hefty rate of interest to the 1% of larger businesses that pay late.

2 Unless an existing contract states otherwise, invoices will have to be settled in 30 days, or the creditor will be able to charge interest at 8% over the Bank of England base rate. For habitually late payers, the penalties should act as a deterrent.

3 According to a survey by Grant Thornton, the speed of payment varies greatly from nation to nation. The Finns settle their invoices in 24 days, the Danes in 35, the Swedes in 37, and the Germans in 38. In the UK creditors must wait almost a fortnight longer – the average payment period is 50 days. Still worse, a NatWest survey of small businesses found that one in 10 of them had 30% of their invoices

unpaid after three months.

4 The Bill sounds like a good idea, but the small business community have their doubts. 'We are sceptical,' says a spokesman from the Federation of Small Businesses. 'Most people won't impose interest, and on the continent,* legislation hasn't made much difference.' In fact, some European late payment legislation has failed. For example, in Italy the average payment wait is 84 days. The Federation aims to use the Bill to raise awareness about the effects

of late payment. It will publish its first league table* of worst payers, compiled by Dun & Bradstreet, in the autumn and believes this naming and shaming exercise will have more impact than the legislation.

* *Name, shame and claim:* to cause embarrassment (shame) to companies that pay late by making it known that they pay late
* *a bill:* a proposal for a new law
* *on the continent:* continental Europe
* *league table:* a public list of all the worst payers

The Express

3 Read paragraph four and answer the questions.

1 What is the response from the small business community?

2 What example does the spokesman from the Federation of Small Businesses use to support his opinion?

3 How will the Federation use the new law?

4 What will it publish soon and why?

**Language
Focus Two**

Gerunds and infinitives

1 When there are two verbs together in a sentence, the second verb
sometimes takes the infinitive and sometimes takes the gerund (...*ing* form).
Read the sentences and complete the rules.

> Please **consider introducing** an ethical policy.
>
> He **agreed to introduce** an ethical policy.
>
> We **must introduce** an ethical policy.
>
> 1 After the verb consider, we use _____
>
> 2 After the verb agree, we use _____
>
> 3 After the modal verb must, we use _____

2 It is difficult to remember if a verb is followed by
a gerund or an infinitive. A good dictionary, such
as the *Longman Active Study Dictionary*, or the
higher level *Longman Business English Dictionary*,
shows you which form a second verb takes.

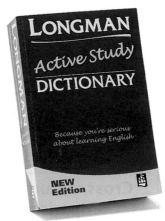

agree /əˈgriː/ v **1** [I,T] to have the
same opinion about something: **+ with**
*I agree with Karen. It's much too
expensive.* | **+ that** *Everyone agreed
that the new rules were stupid.* | **+
about/on** *My first husband and I never
agreed about anything.* → opposite
DISAGREE **2** [I,T] to make a decision
together after discussing something:
agree to do sth *They agreed to share the
cost of the party.* | **+ on** *We're still try-
ing to agree on a date for the wedding.*
| **+ that** *It was agreed that Mr Rollins
should sign the contract on May 1st.* **3**
[I,T] to say yes when someone sug-
gests a plan or asks you to do something: **agree to do sth** *She agreed to stay
at home with Charles.* | **+ to** *The boss
would never agree to such a plan.* **4** [I]
if two pieces of information agree,
they say the same thing: **+ with** *Your
story doesn't agree with what the
police have said.*

consider /kənˈsɪdə‖-ˈsɪːr/ v **1** [I,T] to
think very carefully about something:
*My client needs time to consider your
offer.* | **consider doing sth** *Have you ever
considered living abroad?* **2** [T] to
remember particular facts or details
when making a decision: *You should
consider the effect the move will have
on your family.* | **+ how/what/who etc**
*Have you considered how hard life is
for these refugees?* **3** [T] to think of
someone or something in a particular
way: **consider sb (to be) sth** *Mrs. Gillian
was considered to be an excellent
teacher.* | **consider sth (to be) sth** *We con-
sider your support absolutely essen-
tial.*

must /məst; *strong* mʌst/ *modal verb*
1 used to say that something is necessary and has to be done: *All passen-
gers must wear seatbelts.* | *You must
not allow your dog out without a
leash.* | *It's getting late, I really must
go.* → see also HAVE[3] **2** used to say
that you think something is very likely to be true: *George must be almost
eighty years old now.* | *That car must
have been going at 90 miles an hour!*
3 used to suggest that someone
should do something: *You must see
Robin Williams' new movie. It's really
funny.*

Which group of verbs is followed by: an infinitive without *to*?
a gerund? an infinitive with *to*? Check in a dictionary.

Group A					
like	dislike	delay	finish	include	avoid
postpone	practise	risk	suggest	involve	

Group B					
arrange	decide	expect	hope	help	manage
promise	plan	refuse	want		

Group C				
can	could	may	might	should

▶ **Grammar Reference page 154**

Language Practice Two

1 **Read the two views on whether companies are responsible. Put the verbs in the correct form.**

DO YOU THINK COMPANIES ARE RESPONSIBLE?	
YES	**NO**
• Many companies understand that their responsibility includes (conduct) [1] _____ their business in an ethical way and in ways that help (preserve) [2]_____ the environment.	• They only introduce ethical policies if they think it will help (improve) [7]_____ their profits.
• Companies know that good practice involves (provide) [3]_____ good working conditions.	• Many companies avoid (give) [8]_____ details of what they are doing.
• Many companies help (raise) [4]_____ money for local communities.	• They refuse (change) [9]_____ their practices.
• Companies agree (introduce) [5]_____ stricter measures to reduce pollution.	• Many companies risk (produce) [10]_____ goods which are harmful in order to make a profit.
• Companies must (make) [6]_____ a profit. If they don't, there will be no jobs for the workforce.	• They must (do) [11]_____ more to reduce damage to the environment.

2 **Work in pairs. Student A:** You think companies are responsible.
Student B: You don't think that companies are responsible.
Prepare your arguments, then close your books and discuss!

Listening

1 **Kevin Manton gives his view on corporate responsibility. Before you listen, work in groups and discuss the three statements. Do you agree with any of them?**

1 Many companies have ethical policies and are responsible in business.

2 If a company wants to be profitable it must appear to be ethical.

3 Companies are non-ethical organisations. To expect them to start being ethical is like expecting lions to become herbivores.

2 🔲 **11.4a Listen to Kevin Manton's answer. Which is his view?**

3 🔲 **11.4 Listen to the whole interview and answer the questions.**

1 What are the three examples of big business not considering the needs of people and environment.

2 Kevin Manton gives four examples of products that he doesn't buy. What are they?

3 He gives three examples of products he always tries to buy. What are they and why does he buy them?

Writing

Both ... and, either ... or, neither ... nor

1 Read the advertisement for Cafédirect and the description of Traidcraft's operations. Both Cafédirect and Traidcraft pay 'first world' prices for 'third world' products.

YOU DON'T GET COCAINE

The coffee growers of Latin America face a problem. **Either** they get paid a fair price for their coffee, **or** they face bankruptcy and may have to turn their land over to the illegal production of the coca plant for cocaine.

Cafédirect helps avoid this problem, because more of the money you pay for Cafédirect roast and ground coffee goes directly to the growers.

The result? They continue to produce high quality Arabica coffee for Cafédirect.

Cafédirect. Fair trade. Excellent coffee.

Traidcraft puts social priorities before profits

Paul Gosling reports

Traidcraft does not claim to offer the best dividends to its shareholders, nor the cheapest prices to its customers, nor the highest wages to its staff.

But the company lacks neither customers nor workers, and volunteers freely give their time to sell its products. The reason? Traidcraft describes itself as a social enterprise, and the first item on the agenda is to promote fair trade with underdeveloped countries.

Notice how *both ... and* is used in this sentence.

Ⓐ **Both** Cafédirect **and** Traidcraft pay 'first world' prices for 'third world' products.

2 The coffee growers of Latin America have two options:
   a to grow coffee   **b** to grow the coca-plant

1 If companies don't pay a fair price for their coffee, what will happen?

2 What does Cafédirect do to avoid this problem?

3 Complete this sentence from the advertisement.

Ⓑ _____ they get paid a fair price for their coffee, _____ they face bankruptcy.

3 Look at the Traidcraft text.

1 Is Traidcraft more focused on profits or on social problems?

2 Why do customers buy its products, and why do shareholders invest in the company?

3 Complete this sentence from the text.

Ⓒ   The company lacks _____ customers _____ workers.

4 Does the company lack workers? Does it lack customers?

4 Look again at the three sentences A, B and C.

1 **Which sentence shows:**

a that there is a quantity of two?

b that there are two possible options?

c that both options are excluded?

2 Is **either ... or** used with a negative or positive verb?

3 Is **neither ... nor** used with a negative or positive verb?

5 Complete the sentences with *both ... and, either ... or, neither ... nor.*

1 Traidcraft does not pay _____ its shareholders _____ its staff very well.

2 Traidcraft offers _____ the best dividends to its shareholders, _____ the cheapest prices to its customers.

3 Companies can choose to pay _____ 'first world' prices _____ 'third world' prices for goods from developing countries.

4 _____ Traidcraft _____ Cafédirect choose to pay 'first world' prices.

6 Combine the sentences. Use *both ... and, either ... or, neither ... nor.*
Example:
Neither Cafédirect nor Traidcraft wants to harm the environment.

1 Cafédirect does not want to harm the environment. Traidcraft doesn't want to harm the environment.

2 Traidcraft is a socially responsible company. Cafédirect is a socially responsible company.

3 We can offer to deliver all the goods next Wednesday. We can send part of the order today and the rest next week.

4 We can withdraw from the market totally. We can concentrate our efforts on a small sector.

5 Brian's application for the job of Ethical Policy Director is very strong. Alec's application is strong. It's a difficult decision.

6 Latin American coffee growers can sell their coffee beans to Cafédirect. Latin American coffee growers can grow the coca plant for cocaine.

7 Traidcraft doesn't find it difficult to recruit voluntary staff. Cafédirect doesn't find it difficult.

► **Grammar Reference page 160**

Business Communication

Negotiating

1 Read the Traidcraft advertisement and complete the job specification.

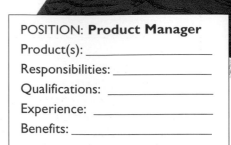
HANDWOVEN
$120

Traidcraft

Traidcraft is a unique company applying Christian principles to bring justice to international trade.

PRODUCT MANAGER
(Fairly Traded Gifts & Homeware)

Your job will be to assist in the management of the Gifts and Homeware business which markets a range of fairly traded products from the 'third world'.

You will be responsible for various aspects of Product Management.

You will be highly motivated and have a degree in Marketing or similar and have one or two years' experience in Product Management.

All jobs have flexible hours and a non-contributory pension scheme.

For further details contact:
Personnel Dept., Traidcraft plc, Kingsway, Gateshead NEH 0NE
Tel: 091 491 059

Traidcraft
Trading for a fairer world

POSITION: **Product Manager**
Product(s): _____
Responsibilities: _____
Qualifications: _____
Experience: _____
Benefits: _____

$20

$9

2 The Product Manager will negotiate with overseas suppliers and agents to buy goods.

1 In your opinion, what skills or personal qualities do you need to be a good negotiator? *compromise...?*

2 What kind of atmosphere should you create for the negotiation? *calm? friendly?*

3 Look at the handmade products below. Is this sort of product popular in your country?

$10

$100

$7

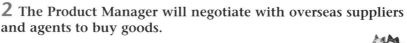
$3

Final Task

4 Work in pairs. Student A is the Product Manager from Tradecraft and is interested in some of the products on page 130. Student B is the agent who represents the producers of these goods.

STUDENT A

Buyer

The agent will visit you and try to persuade you to buy his/her products. You have pictures of the products he/she is offering, with suggested prices. You like the products and decide to buy some of them. You will pay 'first world' prices, but you want to negotiate to get the best price for your company.

Choose the product(s) you would like to buy and decide on the highest price you will pay for each item. Look at page 147 to find out your budget. Prepare for the negotiation.

Useful language:
- *If you ... I'll ...*
- *I'd like both ... and ...*
- *I'm sorry, but I'm afraid that's not acceptable.*

STUDENT B

Agent

You visit the buyer and show him/her the pictures of the products you are offering with suggested prices.

Try to persuade him/her to buy your goods. He/She will pay 'first world' prices, but expect him/her to bargain with you to get a good price for his/her company. He/She has a budget and cannot spend more than this.

Think about what discount you will give if he/she wants to buy in large quantities.

See page 148 to find out the lowest sum you will accept.

Prepare for the negotiation.

Useful language:
- *If you ... I'll ...*
- *I'm sorry, but I'm afraid that's not acceptable.*

$10

Use the points below to write a paragraph about Cafédirect and Traidcraft.

Cafédirect }
Traidcraft }
- do good for the community
- pay first world prices
- don't exploit the workers
- make a profit
- don't pollute the environment

Example:
Both Cafédirect and Traidcraft do good for the community.

Checklist for Unit 11:

1 In the following sentence, is the consequence probably going to happen?
   If our customers continue to pay late we might go out of business.

2 Name three responsibilities that companies have.

3 What pattern follows these verbs? *refuse consider could*

4 Are the following sentences grammatically correct?
   a Both the Cooperative Bank and Friends Provident have a strong ethical policy.
   b Neither the Cooperative Bank nor Friends Provident will invest in companies that cause harm.

5 What is an important grammatical structure to use when you are negotiating?

12 *Competition*

In this unit:

- **Language Focus**
  Present perfect: present result
  Present perfect: unfinished past
  Pronunciation: strong and weak forms of *have*
  /həv//həz/, weak form of *for* /fə/

- **Skills**
  Writing: Curriculum Vitae
  Reading: Pepsi and Coca-Cola
  Listening: competing in a global market

- **Vocabulary**
  Word groups

Key Vocabulary

▭ **12.1** In an **open market** any number of sellers or **competitors** can offer goods for sale. An efficient producer, who keeps costs low, can set a low price for goods that other companies find it difficult to **compete** with. All companies try to gain the biggest **market share** possible, and compete aggressively with their **main competitors** to do this. Companies with the biggest market share for a product, the **market leaders**, may compete with their rivals on quality, image, brand loyalty or price. Major companies compete across borders in the **global market place** to try to **enter new markets** in countries where they do not have a presence.

Lead-in

Japan is one of the most competitive soft drinks markets in the world. There are more than 7,000 different soft drinks on the market and 500 different soft drinks manufacturers. The Coca-Cola Japan Company is the market leader and its product range in Japan includes more than 25 brands and 60 flavours.

1 Work in pairs and discuss the market in a country you know well.

1 How many brands of soft drinks can you name?

2 How many manufacturers can you name?

3 Who are the market leaders or main competitors?

4 Is the soft drinks market very competitive?

2 Who are the main competitors in the market in the following sectors?
sportswear   fashion   cars   telecommunications   computers

3 The global market is very competitive. What can companies do to persuade customers to buy their product instead of another similar one?

**Language
Focus One**

Present perfect: present result of past actions

> The Coca-Cola Company *has formed* a new company, Coca-Cola Beverages (CCB) by the demerger of its bottling businesses in central Europe and Asia. The Coca-Cola company *has floated* 49.9% of the new company's shares on the London stock exchange, and has retained 51.1% of the shares. A survey by Eurominor *has identified* eastern Europe as the fastest growing market for soft drinks, so the fact that CCB is the largest bottling company in central and eastern Europe means the shares should be very popular. The parent company *has split* the existing Asian and central European bottlers to exploit the growth in the European market.

1 Match these three verbs with a synonym.

1 to form (a company)   **a** to divide

2 to retain (shares)   **b** to create

3 to split (the company)   **c** to keep

2 What three things has Coca-Cola done? Complete the sentences with the past participle of one of the verbs.

1 It has _____ a new company (CCB).

2 It has _____ 51.1% of the shares in CCB.

3 It has _____ the Asian and central European bottlers.

3 Why has Coca-Cola split the Asian and central European bottlers?

4 We use the present perfect to connect the past and the present – to say how a past action is significant *now*, or what its present result is.

> **1 Read sentences a and b.**
>
> a *Coca-Cola **has created** a new bottling company.*
>
> We're not interested in **when** the company was created but in the **present result**, i.e. the bottling company is now ready to exploit the growth in the European market.
>
> b *Coca-Cola **has floated** CCB's shares on the London stock exchange.*
>
> We're not interested in **when** Coca-Cola floated the shares but in the **present result**, i.e. we can buy shares in the company now.
>
> **2 What is the present result of these sentences?**
>
> a *The parent company has split the existing Asian and central European bottlers.*
>
> b *Coca-Cola has retained 51.1% of the new company's shares.*
>
> **3 Complete the sentence.**
>
> The present perfect is formed with the present tense of the verb
> [1]_____ and the [2]_____ participle.

▶ **Grammar Reference page 152**

Pronunciation One

Weak and strong forms

🔲 12.2 Listen and note the difference in pronunciation of the words *have* and *has*.

Weak	Strong
It has ('s) been a success.	Yes, it has.
	Has it been a success? No, it hasn't.
What have they agreed?	
They've agreed to a company merger.	
We have ('ve) bought shares.	We haven't.

When do we use the strong form? When do we use the weak form?

Language Practice One

Work in pairs. Who is more successful, you or your partner's rival company?

Student B: Turn to page 149.

Student A: Find out what your competitor has done over the last year using the information below.

Example:
A: *Have you increased sales?*
B: *Yes, we've increased sales by 4.5%.*

Quiz

How competitive are you?

You	Your competitor
Yes, by 5%	increase sales?
Yes, 200,000 new customers	attract new customers?
Yes	maintain customer loyalty?
Taiwan Korea?	enter new markets?
No, but going to	introduce ethical policy?
Yes	update your code of practice?
Yes	send your employees on training courses?
No	sponsor sports events?

To score:
For each thing that you have done and your competitor hasn't done, score 2 points.
For each area where you have achieved more than him/her, score 2 points.
If you have both done something, score 1 point.
If you haven't achieved anything, score 0 points.

Reading   **1** Look at the illustration on page 136. What do you think it shows?

2 The competition between Coca-Cola and Pepsi is fierce. Before you read make predictions. Match the sentence openings 1–4, with the endings a–d.

1 In the USA ...

2 Outside the USA ...

3 In eastern Germany ...

4 In Mexico ...

   a Pepsi has a market share of 33%.

   b Coca-Cola outsells Pepsi by 13:1.

   c there is a 41% to 32% ratio in Coca-Cola's favour.

   d Coca-Cola outsells Pepsi by 3:1.

3 Scan the text quickly and see if you are correct.

4 The magazine article describes the competition between Pepsi and Coca-Cola for new markets. Which were the new markets when the article was written? Can you think of any new markets today?

5 Now read the article again and answer the questions.

1 The text contains a lot of dates and figures. What do these dates refer to?

   a 1897   **b** 1943   **c** 1959   **d** 1972   **e** 1989

2 What do these figures refer to?

   a 3:1   **b** 41%–32% ratio   **c** 80%   **d** $2.5 billion   **e** $112 million
   f 60   **g** 28%–33%   **h** $750 million   **i** 720

6 Work in pairs and discuss.

1 When do you think the article was written? Why? Do you think there have been any changes since the article was written?

2 Do you think the market for Coca-Cola and Pepsi's products has expanded?

3 Do you think that sales of Pepsi have overtaken sales of Coca-Cola?

AFIZZ WITH COMPETITION

Coca-Cola and Pepsi are fighting around the world to gain supremacy in newly open territory

1 COCA-COLA HAS operated outside the U.S. since 1897, at first with only marginal competition from Pepsi, and in the process it has become the world's best-known trademark. More than any other product – even Levi's or McDonald's Big Mac – it is an American emblem*. It is also, a Harvard Business School study has found, the second best-known word in the world – after OK.

2 Today Coke outsells Pepsi around 3 to 1 outside the U.S. The domestic race is closer, with a 41%–32% ratio in Coca-Cola's favor. While Pepsi's parent company makes most of its profit from its snack-food and restaurant operations, Coca-Cola gains 80% of its operating profit from its overseas beverage business. Last year's take in the international soft-drinks race was $2.5 billion for Coke, vs. $112 million for Pepsi.

3 In part, Coca-Cola can thank the U.S. government for its success abroad. During World War II, the U.S. military built more than 60 Coke bottling plants outside the U.S. to supply American troops. This gave the company a leg up* in Europe and Asia once the conflict was over. (In the 1943 North Africa campaign, General Dwight D. Eisenhower communicated in a military cable* with Washington: ON EARLY CONVOY REQUEST SHIPMENT THREE MILLION BOTTLED COCA- COLA, (FILLED) … SHIP WITHOUT DISPLACING OTHER MILITARY CARGO.

4 Pepsi got its international marketing break in 1959 when then

NEUBECKER

chairman Donald Kendall handed Soviet President Nikita Krushchev a bottle as cameras clicked: that gave the company an entree into Eastern Europe. In 1972 Leonid Brezhnev gave Pepsi exclusive franchise in the Soviet Union.

5 Since the collapse of the Berlin Wall in 1989, Coca-Cola has moved swiftly to overcome Pepsi's edge in Eastern Europe. Coke claims the lead in Hungary, Poland, the Czech Republic, Slovakia, Romania, Bulgaria and the former Yugoslavia. Pepsi is fighting especially hard in the former Soviet Union where it claims to retain the lead. Coke, however, now outsells Pepsi by more than 13 to 1 in eastern Germany.

6 Pepsi's strongest recent showing has been in Mexico where the company reports its market share has jumped from 28% to 33% during the past two years. "They're fighting over every extra case*," says consultant Daniel Caraco of Arthur D. Little Mexicana. With its

$750 million investment Pepsi intends to double plant* capacity by 1998.

7 However the Coke-Pepsi battle turns out, people the world over will probably drink more of the beverages. "Both companies are going to make their products more available. They're also going to lower prices. That means more consumers buying more soft drinks," says Joseph Doyle, who follows the industry for Smith Barney in New York City. The average American consumes 720L of soft drinks a year – more soft drinks in fact than water. Non-Americans have a long way to go before they reach that level – and that would translate into booming business for the two giants.

* *emblem:* symbol
* *leg up:* some extra help
* *cable:* cables were used to communicate before telex or fax
* *case:* container
* *plant:* factory

Vocabulary

Word group: competition

1 Do these phrases describe the stronger or the weaker competitor?

> to claim the lead   to outsell   to gain supremacy

2 Complete this sentence using the phrases from the box.

> Both Coca-Cola and Pepsi want to [1] _____ _____
> _____ in the race, to [2] _____ the rival's products in order
> to [3] _____ _____.

Compound nouns and adjectives

Compound nouns and adjectives are words made up of two parts.

1 Work in pairs. Underline the following two-part words in the text.

> **a** best-known (para. 1)   **d** overseas (para. 2)
>
> **b** trademark (para. 1)   **e** soft-drinks (para. 2)
>
> **c** snack-food (para. 2)   **f** chairman (para. 4)

2 Which ones are adjectives and which ones are nouns? What does each word mean?

3 Use each compound word to complete the sentences.

1 Global companies have many _____ branches.

2 Nestlé is well-known for its _____ operations.

3 The UK _____ sector is growing rapidly.

4 A _____ is a symbol used by a company to identify and advertise its goods.

5 OK is the _____ word in the world.

6 The _____ is the most senior person in the company.

Cross-cultural Comparison

1 Is Pepsi or Coca-Cola more dominant in your home market? Can you think of reasons why?

2 What tactics do they use to increase sales?

3 What other very competitive markets are there in your country? (e.g. chocolates and sweets, fast food). Who are the main competitors?

4 Do you think these companies behave responsibly in their attempt to outsell their competitors?

Listening

1 📼 **12.3a Listen to Keith Jackson talking about competition in a global market. Note the definitions of three strategies for becoming a market leader.**

1 Cost focus   _____

2 Differentiation _____

3 Innovation   _____

2 📼 **12.3b Keith talks about the strategies of different companies selling soft drinks. Listen and complete the table.**

Supermarket brand cola

COMPANY	STRATEGY	HOW THEY EMPLOYED THE STRATEGY
1 Safeway Tesco Sainsbury }	cost focus	
2 Tango	differentiation	
3 Virgin Cola	innovation	

3 📼 **12.3c Keith talks about problems for companies who compete in the global market place. Make notes about McDonald's under the following headings.**

1 Quality: _____

2 Local culture and customer expectations: _____

3 Marketing: _____

4 The product: _____

Language Focus Two

Present perfect: unfinished past

> Coca-Cola *has been* the number one soft drink in France *since* 1966. In other words, it *has been* the market leader *for* around *40 years*. Today, French consumers drink an average 88 servings of Coca-Cola products each year.

We use the present perfect to focus on an action or state which started in the past and continues up to the present.

1 Is Coca-Cola the number one soft drink in France now?

2 Is the company a market leader now?

3 Circle which time markers we use to show:

    a the starting point of the action or state?   *for/since*

    b the period of time between the start of the action/state and now?   *for/since*

4 Which time marker do we use with each of the following?

    a 1967   b a long time   c December   d three weeks   e a month

 **Grammar Reference page 152**

Pronunciation Two

Weak form of *for* /fə/

[cassette] 12.4 Listen to these three sentences. How is the time marker *for* pronounced? Practise saying them the same way.

Language Practice

1 Work in pairs. Complete each sentence with the present perfect of the verb in brackets and a time marker – *for* or *since*.

1 Coca-Cola (have) _____ bottling plants outside the US _____ World War II.

2 Pepsi (be) _____ successful in Eastern Europe _____ 1959.

3 Pepsi (have) _____ an exclusive franchise in the Soviet Union _____ 1972.

4 Coca-Cola and Pepsi (be) _____ in competition _____ many years.

5 Coca-Cola (outsell) _____ Pepsi in many Eastern European countries _____ the collapse of the Berlin Wall.

6 Supermarkets (produce) _____ their own brands of cola _____ the last decade.

7 The Coca-Cola recipe (not change) _____ _____ 1886.

2 Cable & Wireless is one of the world's leading suppliers of telecommunications services.

Use the prompts to write a paragraph about the company.

- C&W – maintain a presence in the Arabian Gulf – 1870, and today views the region as one of top growth potential

- C&W – operate – Asia – over 100 years

- In the Caribbean C&W – supply international connections – over a century. They – run – domestic as well as international systems – 1980s

- C&W – operate in the UK – the 1980s

3 Work in pairs and take it in turns to find out more about your partner.

Example:
'Are you working at the moment as well as studying?'
'Yes, I am. I work for ...'
'How long have you worked there?'
'For about three months/since January.'

Ask about:

- work (where? how long?)

- where he/she lives (where? how long?)

- hobbies he/she has (what? how long?)

- study English (how long?)

Writing Preparing for a job: CVs and interviews

You want a job. Answer the following questions.

How do you give yourself a competitive edge?

1 Have you decided what sort of job you really want?   Yes/No
2 Have you spoken to anyone who does the sort of job you would like to do?   Yes/No
3 Have you found out about the companies you would like to work for?   Yes/No
4 Have you spoken to anyone who works for these companies?   Yes/No
5 Do you know what skills you have gained and the skills you have lost in recent years?   Yes/No
6 Have you done anything in the last year which has developed your skills?   Yes/No
7 Do you regularly read the business pages of newspapers or professional journals?   Yes/No
8 Have you talked to a recruitment agency that specialises in your area of work?   Yes/No
9 Have you written or updated your Curriculum Vitae in the last six months?   Yes/No

Score

Yes = 1 point   No = 0 points

0–3   You need to spend more time on preparing yourself for a new job.

4–6   You have made a good start, but you still need to do more work to stand out from the competition.

7–9   You are in a strong position to get a new job.

1 Whatever your score in the quiz, your CV can put you in a strong position.

Your CV should be:
- word-processed
- laser printed on good quality paper
- no longer than two pages of A4 paper

You should include:

1 **Personal details**
   The employer wants to know who you are and how to contact you (essential information only).

2 **Education**

3 **Work experience** Don't just describe the job – stress what you achieved and what you learnt.

4 **Positions of responsibility**
   If you do not have a lot of work experience, this section will show employers your potential.

5 **Skills** Be positive about your ability – never undersell your experience.

6 **Interests** Stress any significant achievements related to your interests.

7 **Referees**
   - Current students and recent graduates should choose an academic referee and a personal one (this could be an employer).
   - Get your referees' permission first and tell them what you are applying for and what you would like them to stress in a reference.

2 Read the advice on page 140 and look at Melanie Henderson's CV. Following the guidelines, prepare your own CV.

curriculum vitae

Personal Details

Melanie Henderson

Date of birth
3.11.1978

Address
99 Newlands Park
London
SE30 8UJ
Tel: 0171 25650

Put your most recent studies first.

Education

1997 – present
Degree in French and Film Studies, University of London
Degree performance to date: 2.1
Specialist subjects: British Cinema, The Narrative Technique

1992 – 1997
Royal Latin School, Aylesbury
4 A Levels: French (B), German (C), English (B), Film studies (A)
7 GCSEs: French (A), German (A), English (A), History (B), Art (A), Maths (B), Economics (B)

Don't go too far back in time or leave any gaps.

Work experience

1999
Information Officer, Futuroscope, France
Responsible for dealing with enquiries in a busy office, responding to 2,000 enquiries a week. This demonstrated my ability to retain a professional approach and a sense of humour while working under pressure.

Put your most recent experience first.

1998
Customer Services Assistant
Provided support for customer enquiries. Dealing with customers' complaints demonstrated my ability to remain calm under pressure. Explaining complex issues simply and clearly helped me to develop my communication skills.

Give more detail about more relevant experience.

Positions of responsibility

In my final year at school, I helped organise a careers fair for all final year students.

Miss this section out if you haven't had a position of responsibility.

Skills

Good working knowledge of Microsoft Word and Excel Spreadsheets
Working knowledge of French and Italian
Current clean driving licence

Don't just list your interests – add a few details.

Interests

Travel: I have travelled extensively and independently in Europe.
Music: I play the guitar in a semi-professional band and have done a number of 'gigs' for school and student clubs.

Give two referees.

Referees

Hamish Roberts
(Tutor at University of London)
17 Woodland Avenue
Oxford
OX11 7GGR

Richard Gayle
(Customer Services Manager/DAT)
31 Pleasant Street
London
SE18 3LSR

Business Communication

Interview skills

1 Read these comments about bad interview experiences and match them with the illustrations. Have you ever had a bad interview experience?

1 'My friend was told that on a scale of good to poor he was at the bottom end of reasonable.'

2 'A friend was asked to make up a song and sing it at an interview with Virgin Atlantic. She did, and got the job.'

3 'I was asked to get on a desk and dance.'

2 A good interview is always well-structured. Work in pairs and put the list of things that an interviewer should do into a logical sequence.

a answer questions ☐

b ask questions about candidate's CV ☐

c explain the plan of the interview ☐

d explain what happens next ☐

e hold a few minutes of neutral conversation ☐

f listen ☐

g make the candidate feel at ease ☐1

h observe ☐

i summarise the main points ☐

3 Work in pairs and decide what the interviewer and the interviewee could say at each of the nine stages.

Example:

1 *Make the candidate feel at ease:*

Interviewer: 'Thank you for coming, I hope you had a good journey.'
Interviewee: 'Yes, thanks. It only took 40 minutes, door-to-door, and it's easy to get here from the station.'

4 ▣ 12.5 At an interview it is important to 'sell' yourself to the company. Listen and write down what each candidate says to sell him/herself.

Brett

Barry

Julie

5 Work in pairs, and roleplay this job interview at a soft drinks company.

STUDENT A

You work for a soft drinks company and want to recruit some energetic, youthful people to your marketing department. Experience is not essential but enthusiasm and the desire to learn is.

Read Student B's Curriculum Vitae, then prepare to interview him/her.

Make sure the interview is well-structured, and that you have a list of questions about the interviewee's CV ready.

STUDENT B

You have applied to a soft drinks company who want to recruit some energetic, youthful people to its marketing department. You are very keen on the job, and think you have a chance because they say that experience is not essential, but enthusiasm and the desire to learn is.

Give Student A your Curriculum Vitae to read, then prepare to be interviewed by him/her.

Prepare a list of subjects that you think the interviewer might ask about and have answers about your CV ready. Plan how to 'sell' yourself at the interview.

Final Task

Work in pairs. Look back through *First Insights into Business* and discuss.

1 What topics have you learnt about?

2 Which ones did you find most interesting?

3 Which companies have you learnt about?

4 Which of the companies would you like to work for and why?

Checklist for Unit 12:

☐ 1 Think of three things that you have learnt about Coca-Cola in this unit.

☐ 2 What tense do we use to talk about the present results of past actions?

☐ 3 What tense do we use when we focus on *when* something happened?

☐ 4 When do we use: *for* + present perfect?

☐ 5 When do we use: *since* + present perfect?

Finance, Corporate Responsibility and Competition

Business Review

Heavenly Chocolate

The Fairtrade chocolate bar 'Divine' is made from West African cocoa beans, grown by farmers who own a one third share in the company and who receive a Fairtrade premium for their produce. One taster asked 'Is it Cadbury'*s?', which pleased Twin, the company that makes 'Divine'. Twin also owns Cafédirect Fairtrade coffee, which showed a 55% growth in sales last year.

Cadbury: large, successful chocolate manufacturer

1 Why are the cocoa bean farmers paid a Fairtrade premium?

2 Why were Twin pleased when a consumer asked 'Is it Cadbury's?'

3 Is the market for Fairtrade coffee healthy? How can you explain this trend?

4 Who are the main competitors in the market for chocolate and coffee? Do you think they need to worry about Fairtrade products?

Vocabulary Review

1 All the words in the box are key words from units 10, 11 and 12. Work in pairs and put each word into the correct list.

1 interest rate	11 enter new markets
2 annual report	12 market leader
3 rise	13 tax year
4 market share	14 turnover
5 offshore bank account	15 society
6 profit and loss account	16 global market
7 financial results	17 open market
8 payment on time	18 fall
9 ethical consumers	19 competitors
10 product policy	20 environment

Finance	Corporate Responsibility	Competition
_____	_____	_____
_____	_____	_____
_____	_____	_____
_____	_____	_____
_____	_____	_____

2 Give a definition for each word.

3 Can you add other key words from units 10, 11 or 12 to the lists?

Grammar Review

1 Talking about figures and Conditional 1

In its first 100 years Coca-Cola has been adaptable and has responded to market changes. New markets are opening up all the time as the political situation changes around the world. It might seem surprising, but the majority of the world's population hasn't drunk Coca-Cola yet!

The pie chart shows Coca-Cola's target markets.

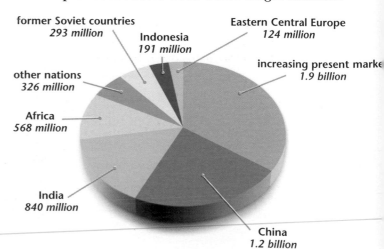

former Soviet countries
293 million

Indonesia
191 million

Eastern Central Europe
124 million

other nations
326 million

increasing present marke
1.9 billion

Africa
568 million

India
840 million

China
1.2 billion

2 Work in pairs and answer the questions.

1 What is the total size of Coca-Cola's potential new market?

2 Which three regions of the world offer Coca-Cola new opportunities and what is the total size of these three?

3 How big is each of the three markets, as a percentage of the whole?

4 What problems might Coca-Cola find in the business environment of these areas?

5 Are there any ethical issues the company should consider when entering these markets?

6 Who will Coca-Cola's main competitors be in these areas?

7 How big is the proposed increase in its present market as a percentage of the whole?

8 What strategies can Coca-Cola use to increase its present market by 1.9 billion?

3 Look at the Conditional 1 sentences which describe the pie chart. Fill the gaps with a verb in the correct form.

1 If Coca-Cola ____ (increase) its present market by 1.9 billion consumers, it ____ ____ (be) the most powerful soft drinks brand in the world.

2 If Coca-Cola ____ (promote) itself successfully in China, its market share ____ ____ (grow) by around 20%.

3 If Coca-Cola ____ (market) itself in China, it ____ have to sell more to earn the same profit as it earns in America because prices will be much lower.

4 If consumption per person ____ (be) as high in its new markets as in its current markets, the company ____ have to open many more bottling plants.

5 If the population in North America and Europe ____ (continue) to shrink, Coca-Cola ____ have to enter new markets in order to keep its profits high.

4 Present perfect, gerunds and infinitives

More and more people are investing their money in companies whose activities do not harm society or the environment. Write five sentences.

Make sure the second verb is in the correct form – *gerund* or *infinitive*.

Example: *Ethical investors **have stopped investing** in companies which are involved in the production of weapons.*

1 companies which are involved in weapons production (stop, invest)

2 companies which are involved in animal testing (avoid, deal)

3 companies which have links with certain political regimes (choose, not to be involved with)

4 companies which bring a direct benefit to society or the environment (prefer, deal)

5 companies which contribute to a sustainable fortune e.g. pollution control, information technology, healthcare and public transport (choose, invest)

Writing Review

Re-phrasing and exemplifying, transitive and intransitive verbs

- Decide if each sentence 1–6 describes transitive or intransitive verbs. Circle the answer.

- Use a re-phrasing or exemplifying connector *(in other words/that means/that is to say)* to complete the other gap.

Example:
*Raise is a **transitive** verb, <u>that means</u> it is followed by a direct object.*

1 Raise is a(n) **transitive/intransitive** verb _____ , it is followed by a direct object.

2 Rise is a(n) **transitive/intransitive** verb _____, it is not followed by a direct object.

3 **Transitive/intransitive** verbs, _____ *rise, fall, bargain, compete, respond* are not followed by a direct object.

4 **Transitive/intransitive** verbs, _____ *pay, publish, expect, spend* are followed by a direct object.

5 **Transitive/intransitive** verbs, _____ verbs that are followed by a direct object, form different sentence patterns to _____ verbs.

6 **Transitive/intransitive** verbs, _____ verbs that are not followed by a direct object, form different sentence patterns to **transitive/intransitive** verbs.

Communication Activities

Unit 2 Business Communication

GROUP 1

GROUP 2

STUDENT B

Look at the chart below which gives information about Edizione Holding. Ask Student A for information to fill in the gaps.

Ask about:

- which sectors Edizione Holding operates in
- the names of the companies

STUDENT D

Look at the chart at the bottom of the page which gives information about Sony. Ask Student C for information to fill in the gaps.

Ask about:

- main areas of business
- the names of the companies

KEY

SECTORS

- ● = MANUFACTURING
- ● = FOOD RETAILING
- ● = REAL ESTATE AND AGRICULTURE
- ● = OTHER SECTORS

edizione holding family tree

1 BENETTON GROUP

4 GRUPPO GS

6 _____

7 INVESTMENT

2 BENETTON SPORT SYSTEM _____

3 _____

5 AUTOGRILL

8 _____

9 _____ _____

10 VOLLEY TREVISTO

11 OTHER MINORITY INTERESTS

SONY

1   **2**   **3**   **4**   **5**   **6**

1 _____
a audio
b video
c _____
d information and communication
e electronic components

2 GAME
a Sony Computer Entertainment
b _____
_____
_____

3 MUSIC
a Sony Music Entertainment (Japan) inc.

4 PICTURES
a Sony Pictures Entertainment
b theatre operations

5 _____
a Sony Life Insurance Company Ltd

6 OTHER
a Customer Financing
b _____

Unit 3 Cross-cultural Comparison

Quiz key: aT, bF, cF, dF, eT, fT, gF, hT, iF, jT

Unit 4 Business Communication

STUDENT B

You work with Student A. Your partner is asking you for help with some problems. Make some recommendations.

Now change roles and ask your partner for help with the following situations.

1 Your colleague is preparing a presentation to a group of prospective new clients.
2 Your company, based in Europe, is opening a branch in Brazil.
3 The computers in the sales department are out of date.
4 The number of customer complaints is increasing.

Unit 5 Writing

Student B: Ask and answer questions to find out the history of EMI's products.

Example:
What did EMI do in 1952?
When did EMI introduce the first stereo LP recordings?

Unit 10 Business Communication

STUDENT B

You represent Jyske Bank. Student A is interested in opening a No. 1 account in Gibraltar. Tell Student A what the benefits of the account are, especially the ability to transfer between 25 different currencies. Answer his/her questions and try to persuade him/her to open an account. You are:

• 100% sure: the euro is an excellent business opportunity.
• 100% sure: your account managers will not make mistakes.
• 75% sure: you will double an investment in 10 years.
• 50% sure: interest rates will go up soon.
• 0% sure: the currency market won't crash.

Unit 11 Final Task

Student A: You have a budget of $500.

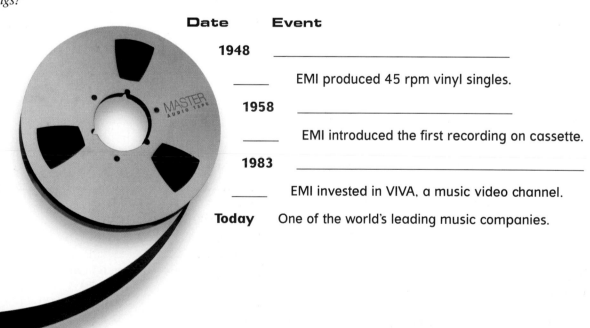

Date	Event
1948	_____
_____	EMI produced 45 rpm vinyl singles.
1958	_____
_____	EMI introduced the first recording on cassette.
1983	_____
_____	EMI invested in VIVA, a music video channel.
Today	One of the world's leading music companies.

Unit 7 Business Communication

Group B

Look at the advertisement for the Memo Recording Pen which *Time* magazine is offering as a free gift. Complete the summary chart.

YOURS
FREE

THE TIME MEMO RECORDING PEN

Record your ideas, thoughts, messages and reminders at the touch of a button with this clever memo pen. With crisp, clear sound and instant playback, it's ideal for the office, when you travel or even at home. And with a single twist it's a handy ballpoint pen.

Measures 147mm x 13mm

TIME

MEMO RECORDING PEN

Appearance: slim and stylish

Special features:	**Benefits:** _____
• two functions:	_____
1 recorder	
2 _____	**Price:** _____
• crisp, clear _____	
• instant _____	

Unit 11 Final Task

Student B: The lowest you will accept is $450.

Unit 8 Language Practice Two

STUDENT B

Student A phones you to ask you about the job you are advertising for an IT research assistant. Use the information below to answer Student A's questions. Use the future form *will*.

• First year: on and off the job training, leading to early responsibility.
• Lots of foreign travel, but not in first year
• Opportunities to spend time in South American or European subsidiaries, but not in first year.
• Interviews: 6 January

Unit 9 Final Task

STUDENT B

Look at the graph which shows cinema attendance for France and Italy.

• Describe the trend to your partner.
• Ask him/her about attendance in Poland, Germany, and Britain.

Complete the graph.

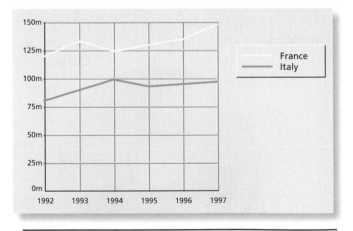

Unit 10 Pronunciation

Student B

a 15.8.2004	**e** 65 cm
b 99kg	**f** 2.30
c 19.9.1960	**g** €5,000,000
d 21.40	**h** $40

Unit 10 Business Communication

STUDENT A

You are interested in opening a No. 1 Account in Gibraltar. Student B works for Jyske Bank and you have an appointment to see him/her about it. You know that the account lets you transfer your money between 25 different currencies.

Ask Student B questions using expressions of probability about:

- the euro – a good investment opportunity?
- Account Managers – well-informed? Will they make mistakes?
- the account – profitable?
- interest rates – changeable?
- currency market – stable?

Decide if you want to open the account or not.

Review 2 Business Communication

STUDENT B

Student A telephones you and asks to speak to the Head of Sales who is not in the office at the moment, so you offer to take a message. Customer Care is very important to your company so you want to give your partner a good impression.

- Explain that the head of sales is not available and ask if you can take a message.
- Find out your caller's name, and a contact number for him/her.
- Ask what message the caller wants to leave
- Get details of the product, i.e. price, designs and colours.

Prepare the call then wait for the phone to ring! Be careful with telephone language, and ask your partner to spell things if necessary.

Unit 12 Language Practice One

Student B

Find out what your competitor has done over the last year using the table below. Ask and answer questions.

Example:
  A: *Have you increased sales?*
  B: *We've increased sales by 5%.*

Quiz

How competitive are you?

You	Your competitor
Yes by 4.5%	increase sales?
Yes 220,000 new customers	attract new customers?
Yes	maintain customer loyalty?
Mexico, Czech Republic	enter new markets?
Yes	introduce ethical policy?
No, but going to	update your code of practice?
Yes	send your employees on training courses?
Yes. Local football team	sponsor sports events?

To score:
For each thing that you have done and he/she hasn't done, score 2 points.
  For each area where you have achieved more than him/her, score 2 points.
    If you have both done something, score 1 point.
      If you haven't achieved anything, score 0 points.

Grammar Reference

VERBS

❶ TENSES

Present simple

USE

We use the present simple to talk about facts or permanent activities:

> *The company has 1,000 employees worldwide.*
> *The staff aren't very friendly.*
> *What does this company do?*

FORM

Positive and negative		
I/you/we/you/they	work	don't work
he/she/it	works	doesn't work

Question		
Do	I/you/we/you/they	work?
Does	he/she/it	work?

⚠ Add *s* or *es* in 3rd person singular
e.g. *she works, he watches*

* We add *es* /ɪz/ when the verb ends in:
  /s/ /z/ /ʃ/ /tʃ/ /dʒ/

  miss → *misses*   close → *closes*
  finish → *finishes*   watch → *watches*
  manage → *manages*

* Verbs that end in consonant + *y*
  in 3rd person singular change **y** to **i** and add **es**
  carry → *carries*
  worry → *worries*

Irregular present simple

⚠ These verbs are irregular:
  have: *he/she/it has*
  do: *he/she/it does*

 Unit 2 Language Focus, page 16

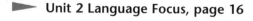

Present continuous

USE

1 We use the present continuous to talk about:
  Things which are happening *at* the time of speaking.

> *I'm trying to call Geoff Peters.*
> *He isn't working today.*
> *What are you doing?*

2 Things which are happening *around* the time of speaking.

> *The company is developing a new drug against asthma.*
> *The company isn't recruiting at the moment.*
> *What are they planning to do?*

⚠ Some verbs are not usually used in the continuous form.

* hear   see   smell   taste
* like   dislike   hate   love   want   wish   hope
* believe   feel (= *think*)   forget   know   mean   remember
* think (= *have an opinion*)   understand
* contain   have (= *own*)
* owe   own   possess

These are **stative verbs**; they describe states or senses.

FORM

be + _____ ing

Positive and negative			
I	am/'m	am not/'m not	flying
you/we/you/they	are	are not/aren't	flying
he/she/it	is	is not/isn't	flying

Question		
Am	I	flying?
Are	you/we/you/they	flying?
Is	he/she/it	flying?

* Verbs that end in a consonant followed by *e*
  take → *take* → *taking*
  manage → *manage* → *managing*

BUT

* Verbs that end in vowel + *e*
  agree → *agreeing*,   see → *seeing*

* Vowel + consonant → double consonant

When the last syllable is stressed, we usually double the final consonant.

fit → *fitting*
be'gin → *beginning*
con'trol → *controlling*

 Unit 2 Language Focus, page 16

Present continuous for future

USE

We use the present continuous to talk about fixed future arrangements.

We're meeting colleagues from the Madrid office on Monday.
I'm not visiting the offices in Athens on this trip.
Are they flying to Heathrow?

➤ **Unit 3 Language Focus, page 24**

➤ **Compare with *going to* below**

Going to

USE

We use *going to* to talk about what we want to do or intend to do in the future. Plans may or may not already be made.

I'm going to spend some time in the UK to improve my English.
I'm not going to take that low-paid job.
What are you going to do at the end of the training course?

FORM

be + going + infinitive with to

Positive and negative

I	am	'm not	
you	are	aren't	
he/she/it	is	isn't	going to apply
we/you/they	are	aren't	

Question

Am	I	
Are	you	
Is	he/she/it	going to apply?
Are	we/you/they	

➤ **Compare with present continuous for fixed arrangements above**

➤ **Unit 8 Language Focus One, page 83**

Will

USE

We use *will* to talk in general terms about the future, not about a particular time in the future.

The training programme will teach you about organisations.
"I'll be here to answer any questions," she said.
We will not discriminate against you.

You won't be disappointed.
Will I get any training?

➤ **Compare with *going to* and present continuous for future above**

FORM

will + infinitive without to

Positive and negative

I/you/he/she/ we/you/they	will/'ll	will not/won't	go

Question

Will	I/you/he/she/it/we/you/they	go?

- *Will* is a modal verb, so the form is the same for all subjects: *I, you, he she, it* etc.

Positive

- We usually use the shortened forms *'ll* and *won't* in speech, but we use *will* and *will not* in writing.

  "I'll deal with this application," she said.
  There will be an introductory talk for new recruits.

  "Don't worry, there won't be a written test, just an oral one."
  We will not ask you to do a written test on this occasion.

➤ **Unit 8 Language Focus Two, page 86**

➤ **Conditional 1, Grammar Reference page 152**

Past simple

USE

We use the past simple to describe things that happened in the past and finished at a specific time.

He started the company in 1969.
They didn't make a profit in the first year.
Did she work there in 1975?

We often use a time reference which refers to the finished event. e.g. *yesterday, last week, last night, three years ago, in 1969, in the first year.*

FORM

> verb stem + *ed*

Positive and negative		
I/you/he/she/it/they/we/you	arrived	didn't arrive

Question		
Did	I/you/he/she/it/they/we/you	arrive?

- verbs that end in *e*
  arrive + **d** → *arrived*
- verbs that end in consonant + **y**
  study → *studied*

⚠ Many past simple forms are irregular.

go: *went*   have: *had*
see: *saw*   buy: *bought*

The verb *to be*

Positive and negative		
I/he/she/it	was	was not/wasn't
you/we/they	were	were not/weren't

Question	
Was	I/he/she/it?
Were	you/we/you/they?

► Irregular verbs page 161

► Unit 5 Language Focus, page 47

Present perfect

USE

We use the present perfect to talk about:

1 How a past action has consequences in the present.

   The two companies have merged.
   Past action: *They merged.*
   Present result: *There is one company now.*

   We've opened a new office in Paris.
   Past action: *We opened a new office.*
   Present result: *We've got a new office in Paris.*

2 An action or state which started in the past and still continues.

   The company has had an office in Moscow since 1992.
   Past starting point: 1992. *The company had an office in Moscow in 1992.*
   Present: *The Company has an office in Moscow.*

   She has worked for the family business for 35 years.
   Past: *She started working 35 years ago.*
   Present: *She is still working there now.*

FORM

> *have* + past participle

Positive and negative			
I/we/you/they/he/she/it	have has	haven't hasn't	looked gone

Question		
Have	I/you/we/you/they	looked? gone?
Has	he/she/it	looked? gone?

⚠ **Note:** The past participle form does not change to match the person.

*He has **looked**.   I have **looked**.*

The past participle of some verbs is irregular.

► Irregular Verbs page 161

► Unit 12 Language Focus One and Two, pages 133 and 138

Conditional 1

USE

We use Conditional 1 to talk about future situations the speaker thinks are probable, and their consequences.

Probable actions	Consequence
If **I sell** soon,	I'**ll get** a better price.
If you **introduce** animal testing,	we **won't buy** from you.
If we **become** environmentally friendly,	**will** you **invest** in us?

Will expresses certainty about the consequence. When we are less sure of the consequence, we can use *may* and *might*.

*If your payment is late, we **may** charge interest.*
*If I don't sell the shares now, **I might** lose money.*

FORM

> *If* + present simple, + *will* + infinitive

Conditional 1 sentences have two clauses. We can start with the *if clause*, or the *main clause*.

If clause	Main clause
If their customers don't pay on time,	their business will suffer.

Main clause	If clause
Their business will suffer	if their customer don't pay on time.

Punctuation
When we start the sentence with the *if* clause, we use a comma (,) before the main clause.

► **Unit 11 Language Focus One, page 121**

⚠ Be careful with third person endings in all main verb tenses.
*she takes, he **is** listening.*

---

❷ MODAL VERBS

We use modal verbs to:

1 give advice and make recommendations. *(should, ought to)*

2 express possibility. *(may, might, could)*

3 talk about the future. *(will)*

Should and *ought to* (recommendations)
USE

We use *should* and *ought to* to recommend change, or to give advice.

*You **ought to** hire a management consultant.*
*They **should** listen to women's views.*
*You **shouldn't** try to change the things you can't change.*
*You **ought not to** postpone the meeting.*
*What **should** we do? / What **ought** we **to** do?*
***Should** we change our code of practice?*
***Ought** we **to** change our code of practice?*

FORM

should + infinitive without to
ought to + infinitive without to

Should

Postive and negative			
I/you/he/she/ we/you/they	should	should not/shouldn't	go

Question		
Should	I/you/he/she/it/we/you/they	go?

Ought to

Postive and negative			
I/you/he/she/ we/you/they	ought to	ought not to	go

Note: We do not usually use *ought to* for questions. We use *should*.

He ought to go.
BUT
Should he go?

⚠ Modal verbs never change their form. We do not add *s̷* in the 3rd person singular form, or tense markers with modal verbs.
He should̷ solve the problem.

► **Unit 4 Language Focus, page 38**

May, *might*, and *could* (possibility)
USE

We use these modal verbs to suggest possible reasons for something, or to speculate.

*The company is now very successful. This **may be** because its markets have more money to spend. Or it **might be** because it is under new management.*

*Prices are higher in the UK. This **could be** because labour costs are high.*
***Could** this **be** the reason?*

⚠ We do not use *may* in the question form to speculate. We use *could*.

~~May it be expensive because labour costs are high?~~

***Could** it **be** expensive because labour costs are high?*

► **Adverbs of certainty, Grammar Reference page 159**

FORM

May, might, could + infinitive without to

Positive			
I/you/he/she/it/we/you/they	may		
	might	be (late)	
	could		

Question		
Might	I/you/he/she/it/we/you/they	be (right)?
Could		

► **Unit 9 Language Focus One, page 95**

► *Will* **Grammar Reference page 151**

Modal verbs for Future possibility

We also use *may*, *might* and *could* to talk about future possibilities.
Might and *could* express a lower probability than *may*.

*I **may** open an account with the Jyske bank.*
*Things are not going well for the company this year, but we **might** be in profit.*
*The share price **could** fall, but I don't think it will.*

► **Unit 10 Business Communication, page 118**

❸ ACTIVE AND PASSIVE VOICE

Active voice

We use the **active** voice to say what people and things **do**.

*The computer **converts** sounds into text.*
*The workers **are demanding** a pay increase of 7%.*

Passive voice

We use the **passive** to say what happens to people and things.

*The sounds **are converted** into text.*

The passive is formal and is often used in report writing.

*The staff **were asked** for their opinions about the catering provision.*

Present simple passive

USE

*Jeans **are sold** all over the world.*
*The car parts **are not assembled** at the Longbridge plant.*
***Is** the report **written** in English?*

We use a passive sentence:

1 when we are interested in who or what acts.

2 when it is obvious who or what does the action so it is unnecessary to say.

FORM

be + past participle

Positive and Negative

I	am/'m	am not/'m not	
you	are/'re	are not/aren't	
he/she/it	is/'s	is not/isn't	invited
we/you/they	are/'re	are not/aren't	

Question

Am	I	
Are	you	
Is	he/she/it	invited?
Are	we/you/they	

We form the present passive with the present simple of the verb *to be* and the *past participle*.

⚠ **Note:** The present passive is usually only used with *it* and *they* – for things rather than people.

They are manufactured in Italy.
It is bought mainly by women.

For regular verbs, the past participle is the same as the past simple form.

➤ **Irregular past participles page 161**

Word order

| | SUBJECT | | OBJECT | |

Active: (The workers) assemble (the car parts) at the Longbridge plant.

| | SUBJECT |

Passive: (The car parts) are assembled at the Longbridge plant.

➤ **Unit 9 Language Focus Two, page 99**

---

❹ GERUNDS (...ing) AND INFINITIVES

When there are two verbs together in a sentence, we must be careful about the form of the second verb.

• After most verbs we use the infinitive with *to*.
  *The company **agrees** to change its ethical policy.*

• After some verbs we use the gerund *-ing* form.
  *We **considered making** the changes last month.*

• After modal verbs we use the infinitive without *to*.
  *They **should** change their policy.*

Some common verbs which are followed by the gerund are:

start begin stop finish delay continue practise imagine consider risk avoid delay involve

➤ **Unit 11 Language Focus Two, page 126**

---

❺ TRANSITIVE AND INTRANSITIVE VERBS

Many verbs are followed by an object e.g.

improve something, *pay* something, *raise* something

These are called **transitive** verbs.

Verb	Object
They improved	the *working* conditions.
They paid	our invoice.
He raised	the question of payment.

Intransitive verbs do not take an object.
e.g. fall, rise, arise

*Our profits **are falling**.*
*Yesterday interest rates **didn't rise**.*
*How did the problem **arise**?*

➤ **Unit 10 Language Focus Two, page 115**

SENTENCES AND CLAUSES

❶ DIRECT AND INDIRECT QUESTIONS

USE

We usually use direct questions to get information.

How much does it cost?
Does the company have a code of practice?

We use indirect questions to ask 'difficult' or personal questions or when we want to be polite.

Could you tell me what qualifications you have?
Can you tell me where I go to get a refund?

FORM

Direct questions: present simple tense

We form direct questions with the auxiliary *do*.

*Where **do** you shop?*

⚠ BUT we do not use the auxiliary *do* with the verb *to be*.

*Where **is** the customer service desk?*

Wh-/How questions

Question words	auxiliary verb	subject	verb
How much	does	it	cost?

with *be*

Question words	verb	subject
How much	is	it?

Yes/No questions

aux	subject	verb
Do	I/you/we/you/they	work?
Does	he/she/it	work?

with *be*

to be	subject	
Am	I/you/we/you/they	OK?
Is	he/she/it	OK?

Indirect questions: present simple tense
Wh-/How questions

polite introduction	question word(s)	subject	verb
Could you tell me	how much	it	costs?

with *to be*

polite introduction	question word(s)	subject	verb
Could you tell me	how much	it	is?

Yes/No questions

polite intro	if	subject	verb
Could you tell me	if	I/you/we/you/they	work?
Could you tell me	if	he/she/it	works?

In indirect *Yes/No* questions we use *if*.

► **Unit 1 Language Focus, page 6**

❷ CLAUSES

Sentences can consist of one clause, e.g.

I'm very pleased.

We often make sentences with two or more clauses.

1 **Main clause (main idea)**
   There are delays with the mail order catalogue …

   Subordinate clause (develops the idea)
   … because we are having problems with the new IT system.

2 We can join two **equal clauses**.
   *I'm really disappointed about the delays **and** Henry is furious.*

Clauses of purpose
USE

Clauses of purpose answer the question *Why?* or *What for?* They are subordinate clauses.

*We are doing it now **to avoid** problems in the future.*
*I need to reduce costs **in order to keep** within the budget.*
*I need to reduce the costs **in order not to go** over budget.*
*We need to make changes to our advertising **so that** we **appeal** to a younger audience.*

He is bringing in a more experienced manager in order that they don't lose more time and money.

In order that and *in order to* are more formal than *to* and *so that*.

FORM

1 To introduce a clause of purpose we use:
   to + infinitive
   in order (not) to + infinitive
   so that + subject + verb
   in order that + subject + verb

Negative
The negative of *to* is *in order not to*.

I'll write it down in order not to forget it.

To make a negative of *so that* and *in order that*, we must change the second clause:

We are buying new software so that we won't have to do so much paperwork.
He's leaving early in order that he won't miss the plane.

 **Unit 4 Writing, page 42**

Defining relative clauses

These clauses give important information about the noun.

*A retailer is a person **who/that** buys goods from the manufacturer.*
*This is the department store **which/that** Peterson owns.*

We choose a relative pronoun depending on whether the noun is a person or a thing

Person	thing(s)
who	
that	that
	which
	(place) where
	(time) when

▶ **Unit 6 Language Focus Two, page 63**

Clauses of cause

These conjunctions (linking words) introduce a clause of cause or reason. They answer the question *Why?*

| because   as   since |

The conjunctions link cause and effect *within* one sentence. They can come in mid position or at the start of the sentence.

Effect		Cause
Main clause	**Conjunction**	**Clause**
He had to go to the USA …	because as since	… no one backed him in the UK.

	Cause	Effect
Conjunction	**Clause**	**Main clause**
Because … As …	no one backed him in the UK	he had to go to the USA.

▶ **Unit 7 Writing, page 76**

Clauses of contrast

Clauses of contrast give information that surprises, or contrasts with the main clause.

Main clause	Clause of contrast
There are more men than women in very senior jobs …	… although there are many women in business.

We use the conjunctions *although, however* and *but* to show contrast between ideas.

| although   but   however |

Notice that they use different grammatical structures.

although
***Although** it's late, I'm still at the office.*
*I'm still at the office **although** it's late.*

but
*I like her style, **but** I don't like her ideas.*

***But** is a co-ordinating conjunction and joins two contrasting ideas of equal importance. It comes in the middle of the two ideas.

however
*The new MD is a woman. **However**, her management style is quite masculine.*
*The new MD is a woman. Her management style, **however**, is masculine.*

However is formal. It contrasts the idea in the second sentence with the idea in the first sentence.

▶ **Unit 8 Writing, page 91**

---

❸ SEQUENCE MARKERS AND CONNECTORS

Sequence markers

We use sequence markers to list and sequence things.

First   First of all   Firstly
Second   Secondly   Third   Thirdly
Then   After that   Next
Lastly   Finally
Now/today (for current situation)

When we list ideas or arguments we usually use:
firstly, secondly, thirdly, lastly, finally

*There are a number of reasons for this: **firstly** the economy is weak, **secondly** labour costs are high and **finally** there is strong competition.*

When we talk about actions we usually use:
first (of all), then, next, after that, next.

***First of all** they designed a new type of shoe, **then** they found a manufacturer to make it. **After that** they started to export it.*

WORD ORDER

In order to make the sequence of actions clear we often start the sentence or clause with the sequencing word.

***First of all** they invented the shoe. **Then** they took their design to a shoe manufacturer.*
***Firstly** I'd like to look at the company history, **then** I'd like to look at the present situation and **lastly** I'd like to talk about our plans for the future.*

▶ **Unit 5 Writing, page 52**

Connectors of effect

The following phrases introduce effects or consequences.

as a result
therefore
so

They link a cause and an effect.

Cause	Effect
The product was too expensive.	As **a result,** sales were poor.
	Sales **therefore** were poor. OR **Therefore,** sales were poor.

As a result, and *therefore* link two sentences. They occur in the second sentence and refer back to the first sentence.

So is a conjunction and links cause and effect in one sentence, telling you what the effect is.

Cause	Effect
The product was too expensive	**so** sales were poor.

 Unit 7 Writing, page 76

Connectors to show additional information

We use these connectors to give additional information.

too/as well
also
in addition

too/as well
Labour costs are high. Inflation is high as well/too.
We use *too* or *as well* at the end of a clause.

also
We use *also* to link two pieces of information.

⚠ *Also* usually comes before the second verb.
The country has high inflation and it also suffers from high unemployment.

When the verb is *to be* we put *also* **after** the verb.
Marks and Spencer is a successful company. It is also a very large company.

in addition
We usually use *in addition* at the start of a second clause.

Clause 1	Clause 2
The company is opening five branches this year	… and **in addition** it is hoping to open two more in Japan next year.

 Unit 9 Writing, page 98

Connectors for rephrasing and giving examples

Rephrasing
It is sometimes useful to say the same thing in two different ways. We can use the following expressions to introduce explanations.

in other words
that is to say
i.e. (in writing only)

in other words
We use *in other words* to introduce a simpler explanation of the previous clause or sentence. We use it at the start of a sentence or clause.
Profit is 10% above the figure at the same time last year. **In other words,** *we're doing well.*

i.e.
We use *i.e.* or *that is to say* to explain the *exact* meaning of the previous clause.
There is a limit on the amount of money you can invest **i.e. $100,000.**

Giving examples
It can be useful to give examples to make your point clear.

for example   e.g.   such as

for example
This is sometimes written e.g.

Word order
We usually put *for example* before the example:
The euro replaces many currencies, **for example,** *the Deutschmark, the franc, and the lira.*

We can put *for example* after the example.
The euro replaces many European currencies – the Deutschmark, **for example.**

Such as always introduces a noun and comes before the noun.

It shows important information **such as** *turnover, operating profit, etc.*

 Unit 10 Writing, page 113

❹ AVOIDING REPETITION

We can avoid repeating a noun by using these words and phrases:

- *it   they*
- *this   that   these   those   others*
- *one/ones   one of them*

It refers back to singular noun.

DHL is an international air express carrier. It delivers documents and packages all over the world.

They refers back to a plural noun.

There are 300 HMV Group stores around the world. They are located in eight countries.

We use ***this, that, these*** and ***those*** to refer back to:

1 nouns
Many companies are multinationals. These include Daimler Chrysler, Sony, Reuters, etc.

2 whole sentences or clauses
Many people believe companies do not care about the environment. This is not true of companies such as the Body Shop.

one(s)

We use *one* to replace a singular countable noun.

He's looking for a job. He'd like one with Sony.

In the plural we use *ones*.

There are different types of companies. I buy from the ones with a strong code of practice.

one of them:

We use ***one of them*** to replace a singular noun.

Many companies produce jeans. Levis Strauss & Co is one of them. (One company of the many which produce jeans.)

others

We use *others* instead of *other* + plural noun.
*Some companies have a code of practice and **others** (**other companies**) do not.*

➤ **Unit 2 Writing, page 20**

ADJECTIVES AND ADVERBS

❶ ADJECTIVES

Order of adjectives

We often use only one adjective before a noun and it is very unusual to use more than three of them.

When we use more than one adjective before the noun, we usually follow this order:

①	②	③	④	⑤	⑥	
opinion	size	shape	colour	origin	material	noun
smart	big	wide	black	French	leather	**bag**

➤ **Unit 7 Language Focus One, page 71**

Comparatives and superlatives

USE

We use the comparative to compare two items:
The grey suit is smarter than the brown suit.

We use the superlative to compare one item with two or more other items:
The black suit is the smartest.

FORM

Adjectives with one syllable

- We add *-er* to form the comparative and ***the*** + *-est* to form the superlative.
  smart: *smarter, the smartest*

- For adjectives that end in *e*, we add *-r* to form the comparative and *-est* to form the superlative.
  wide: *wider, the widest*

- For adjectives that end in a vowel + consonant we double the consonant.
  big: *bigger, the biggest*

Adjectives with two syllables that end in *y*

- comparative: *y* → *i* + *-er*   *crazier*
  superlative the + *-iest*   *the craziest*

Other two syllable and longer adjectives

- Adjectives form the comparative with ***more*** + ***adjective*** and ***the most*** + ***adjective***, *more stylish, the most stylish/more expensive, the most expensive*

than

We use *than* after a comparative.

*You are smarter **than** him.*

as ... as

To show that two things are equal (or not) we use (***not***) ***as*** + adjective + ***as***.

*He is **as** smart **as** you.*
*He is not **as** smart **as** you.*

To form the opposite of the comparative and superlative forms *more/the most* we can use *less/the least.*

*My job is **less** demanding than yours.* (or – *My job is **not** as demanding as yours.*)
*He has **the least** demanding job.*

 It is unusual to say:
He is less rich than you. or *He is the least rich.*

For adjectives that add -*er*, -*est* we usually use **not as ... as**.

*He is **not as** rich **as** you.*

Irregular adjectives

bad	worse	the worst
good	better	the best

► **Unit 7 Language Focus Two, page 77**

---

❷ ADVERBS
Adverbs of manner
USE

We use adverbs of manner to describe how something happens.
*Sales rose **slightly**.*
*Sales fell **dramatically**.*

FORM

Most adverbs of manner add -*ly* to the adjective
sharp → *sharply*   slight → *slightly*

When an adjective ends -*le*
*le + y → **ly***
considerable → *considerably*

When an adjective ends in -*y*
*y → **ily***
steady → *steadily*

When an adjective ends in -**ic**
*ic → **ically***
dramatic → *dramatically*

Word order
Adverbs that end in -*ly* usually come after the verb.

► **Unit 9 Business Communication, page 104**

Adverbs of certainty
We can use these adverbs to say how sure we are about something.

Probability:

1–50%	50–99%	100% sure
perhaps	probably	definitely
maybe	likely	certainly
possibly		

Maybe/Perhaps *prices are high because labour costs are high.*
*Hamburgers **probably** cost more in the UK because of the cost of labour.*
*The cost will **definitely** increase.*

Word order
Perhaps and *maybe* come at the beginning of a clause.

Perhaps *prices will fall.*
*She is leaving the company, **maybe** because she has been offered another job.*

Possibly, probably, definitely and *certainly* usually go between the auxiliary and the main verb.

*It is **probably** the biggest company in Sweden.*
*We have **certainly** decided on a policy.*

Likely is used in a separate clause.

*It is **likely** that we will be taken over.*

► **Unit 9 Language Focus One, page 95**

► **Unit 10 Business Communication, page 118**

DETERMINERS

❶ INDEFINITE, DEFINITE AND ZERO ARTICLES
a/an
We use the indefinite article, *a/an* before a singular countable noun when we refer to it for the first time.
*I bought **a mobile phone** yesterday.*

the
We use *the* before uncountable, countable, singular and plural nouns:

1 when we use the noun for the second (third, fourth ...) time.
*She works for a multinational company ... **The** company has branches all over the world.*

2 when it is clear from the situation who or what we are referring to.
*Let's get them from **the** supermarket.*

zero article
We do not use an article when we talk about things in general.

1 with uncountable nouns
*It's difficult to get **advice** about this problem.*

2 with plural nouns
***People** want to work.*

Compare this to a particular group of people.
***The** people who I work with enjoy their jobs.*

► **Unit 7 Language Focus One, page 58**

② *BOTH ... AND, EITHER ... OR, NEITHER ... NOR*

both (+ noun) **and** (+ noun)

Both ... and shows that two things, are compared.
Both *Traidcraft* **and** *Cafédirect pay first world prices.*

neither (+ noun) **nor** (+ noun)
We use *neither ... nor* to show two options are
excluded i.e. to say that the two options are not
possible or true.
Neither *Traidcraft nor Cafédirect pays third world prices.*

either (+ clause) **or** (+ clause)
Either... or ... shows one of two possible options.
You can buy **either** *direct from the producer* **or** *from the
shop.*

either (+ noun) **or** (+ noun)
When we use *either ... or* as the subject of the clause,
we use a singular verb.
I don't mind which one you buy, **either** *cotton* **or** *silk* **is**
fine.

▶ **Unit 11 Writing, page 128**

③ NUMERALS

Cardinals

We usually use cardinal numbers to talk about
money and years.

It costs $200 – **two hundred** *dollars.*
2002 **(two thousand and two)** *– the year of the euro.*

We use cardinals to express:

Decimals

We say each number individually after the point.
75.72 – **Seventy-five point seven two.**

When a zero occurs before the point, we say *nought*
e.g. *0.5 –* **nought point five.**

Percentages
We use cardinals to express percentages. Percentages
can include decimals.

0.5% – **Nought point five percent.**

Ordinals

We use ordinal numbers:

1 to talk about dates –
   *The meeting is on 1.7.(***the first** *of July)*

2 to rank items –
   This country ranks **second** *in the world
   competitiveness scoreboard.*

3 to express fractions –

$1/5$ **a fifth**, $1/6$ **a sixth**, $1/8$ **an eighth**, $1/10$ **a tenth**

BUT we say:

$1/4$ a quarter, $1/2$ a half, $3/4$ three quarters.

▶ **Unit 10 Language Focus, page 109**

Guide to pronunciation
VOWELS

/ə/	America, seven, creditor
/æ/	cat, backing
/ʌ/	run, money
/ɑː/	half, market
/e/	any, sell
/ɪ/	quick, profit
/iː/	see, decrease
/ɒ/	boss, job
/ɔː/	forty, export
/ɜː/	early third
/ʊ/	good, should
/uː/	true, unique
/ɪə/	beer, year
/ʊə/	tourist, secure
/eə/	hair, share
/eɪ/	plane, operate
/ɔɪ/	join, employ
/aɪ/	finance, why
/əʊ/	go, overcharge
/aʊ/	out, town

CONSONANTS

/p/	shop, product
/b/	box, job
/f/	five, enough
/v/	video, invoice
/t/	time, debt
/d/	drop, read
/θ/	thing, ethical
/ð/	then, the
/tʃ/	charge, question
/dʒ/	job, strategy
/s/	soft, asset
/z/	rise, business
/ʃ/	shares, ambition
/ʒ/	television, pleasure
/k/	car, black
/g/	goods, bag
/m/	margin, demand
/n/	name, turnover
/ŋ/	long, operating
/h/	hard, who
/l/	live, loyal
/r/	recruit, price
/w/	work, award
/j/	yellow, use

Verb List

Irregular verbs

We can not form the past simple tense of **irregular** verbs by adding -ed.
Verbs which have the same past simple and past participle are in **bold**.

INFINITIVE	PAST SIMPLE	PAST PARTICIPLE	INFINITIVE	PAST SIMPLE	PAST PARTICIPLE
arise	arose	arisen	make	**made**	**made**
be	was/were	been	mean	**meant**	**meant**
beat	beat	beaten	meet	**met**	**met**
become	became	become	pay	**paid**	**paid**
begin	began	begun	put	**put**	**put**
bend	**bent**	**bent**	read	**read**	**read**
blow	blew	blown	ring	rang	rung
break	broke	broken	rise	rose	risen
bring	**brought**	**brought**	run	ran	run
build	**built**	**built**	say	**said**	**said**
buy	**bought**	**bought**	see	saw	seen
can	could/was able	been able	sell	**sold**	**sold**
catch	**caught**	**caught**	send	**sent**	**sent**
choose	chose	chosen	shake	shook	shaken
come	came	come	shine	**shone**	**shone**
cost	**cost**	**cost**	shoot	**shot**	**shot**
cut	**cut**	**cut**	show	showed	shown
deal	**dealt**	**dealt**	shrink	shrank	shrunk
do	did	done	shut	**shut**	**shut**
draw	drew	drawn	sing	sang	sung
drink	drank	drunk	sit	**sat**	**sat**
drive	drove	driven	sleep	**slept**	**slept**
eat	ate	eaten	smell	**smelt**	**smelt**
fall	fell	fallen	speak	spoke	spoken
feel	**felt**	**felt**	spell	**spelt**	**spelt**
fight	**fought**	**fought**	spend	**spent**	**spent**
find	**found**	**found**	spread	**spread**	**spread**
fly	flew	flown	stand	**stood**	**stood**
get	**got**	**got**	steal	stole	stolen
give	gave	given	stick	**stuck**	**stuck**
grow	grew	grown	strike	**struck**	**struck**
have	**had**	**had**	swim	swam	swum
hear	**heard**	**heard**	take	took	taken
hit	**hit**	**hit**	teach	**taught**	**taught**
hold	**held**	**held**	tear	tore	torn
hurt	**hurt**	**hurt**	tell	**told**	**told**
keep	**kept**	**kept**	think	**thought**	**thought**
know	knew	known	throw	threw	thrown
lay	**laid**	**laid**	upset	**upset**	**upset**
lead	**led**	**led**	wake	woke	woken
learn	**learnt**	**learnt**	wear	wore	worn
leave	**left**	**left**	win	**won**	**won**
lose	**lost**	**lost**	write	wrote	written

Look at the following verbs: *forget, forgive, under**stand**, with**draw**.*
They follow the same pattern as the verbs ***get***, ***give***, ***stand*** and ***draw***.

Word List

Tapescripts

Unit 1 *Customers*

1.2 Cross-cultural Comparison

SN = Stephen Nicholl

SN: One thing that does irritate me is when I ask somebody for some information about a product or a service and they don't know the answer, but they don't say 'I'm sorry, I don't know the answer to this, I'll find someone who does know the answer' – they try to answer it themselves and it's really a waste of time for everybody concerned.

1.3 Language Focus

R = Receptionist
TS = Tim Saunders

R: Good afternoon, Hi-tone Health and Fitness Centre. How may I help you?

TS: Oh, hello. I'm thinking of joining a fitness centre. Could you give me some information about Hi-tone?

R: Yes, of course.

TS: So first of all, could you tell me how much it costs?

R: Is it just for you?

TS: Yes.

R: OK. It's £550 for a year and for that you can use all the facilities. We have a fully-equipped gym, saunas, steambaths and a swimming pool and squash courts. And you can pay in monthly instalments if you like.

TS: Right. And what are your opening hours?

R: We're open 7 days a week from 6.30 in the morning to 10 every evening.

TS: OK. And how does it work? I mean, could you tell me what the procedure is.

R: You have a fitness assessment with an instructor, then we design a fitness programme for you... and we review your programme every two months.

TS: That's good. Could you tell me what qualifications your instructors have?

R: Oh, they are all fully qualified and very experienced.

TS: Uh-huh. Do you have fitness classes as well?

R: Yes, we do. We run six different types of fitness class. There's one every evening except Saturdays.

T: Right, and what about the class size? Is there a maximum number in each class?

R: Yes, the maximum number of people in a class is fifteen. But there are usually only about 8 people in a class.

TS: And can I come and see if I like it? Do you offer a free introductory session?

R: Yes, we do. I can book you in for that, if you like.

TS: Yes, thank you. Just one final question. Can you tell me if it's possible to bring guests?

R: Yes when you're a member you can bring one guest. It costs £7.50 a visit.

TS: OK. Can I book an introductory session for next week?

R: Sure. Could you give me your name and a telephone number?

1.5 Language Practice

I = Instructor TS = Tim Saunders

I: Do you do any exercise at the moment?

TS: No, I don't. And the problem is I sit at my desk all day.

I: What are your favourite sports?

TS: I like swimming and I enjoy a game of squash now and again!

I: Could you tell me if you have any medical problems or injuries?

TS: No, I'm very healthy, thank goodness.

I: How often do you want to come to the Centre?

TS: Probably three or four times a week.

I: Can you tell me what your objectives are?

TS: I want to get fit and I want to lose a few kilos too.

I: And what do you do?

TS: I'm a business analyst.

1.6 Listening

Int = Interviewer AH = Ann Hislop
SN = Stephen Nicholl

Int: So, Ann and Stephen. I'd like to ask you some questions about customer service. Are there any companies which you are loyal to?

AH: I am fantastically loyal to Marks and Spencers.

SN: I'm also quite loyal to Marks and Spencers. If you buy presents for people and they don't like them, they can take the things back and they can exchange them

Int: So what's the attitude of the staff like at Marks and Spencer's?

AH: Friendly...

SN: Yeah

AH: ... helpful,

SN: professional

AH: ...co-operative, loyal to their company. They obviously enjoy working there most of the time. Yeah I don't know how they manage it, but they have a very friendly er staff.

Int: What about the quality of their of their products?

AH: Fantastic.

Int: Are there any other companies which you're very loyal to?

SN: One company that I am loyal to, I think, is my bank which is First Direct.

Int: And why's that?

(1.6b) SN: Well, first of all they're extremely convenient to use. I do all my banking is over the phone and I can do this at any time of the day. I can find out how much money there is in my account, I can pay all my bills. I don't I don't send any bills through the mail erm and also they're very very professional, they're very friendly.

1.7 Business Communication

CONVERSATION 1

Secretary: Good morning. RTA, Lisa speaking, how may I help you?

164

Customer: Oh, hello. Erm, I have an appointment to see David Barnes on Tuesday, but I'm afraid I can't make it then. Would it be possible to change it?
Secretary: Just one moment. Er yes, I can give you an earlier appointment, if you like.
Customer: Yes, that would be very helpful. Thank you.

CONVERSATION 2

Secretary: Mr Smith will be with you in a minute. Would you like to take a seat?
Customer: Thank you.
Secretary: Would you like a coffee?
Customer: Thank you very much. That would be very nice. Black, no sugar please.

CONVERATION 3

Secretary: Shall I call a taxi for you?
Customer: That's very kind of you, but I think I'll get some exercise and walk.

Unit 2 *Companies*

2.4 Language Practice

BA = Business analyst
BA: Right, so the first company I want to look at is a pharmaceuticals company. It develops and manufactures a wide range of medicines and it's currently developing a new drug against asthma. Well, as you all know, more and more people are suffering from asthma so they hope to make a healthy profit from this drug.
The company is currently preparing to launch a TV advertising campaign. As you may know, it is illegal to show drugs on TV, so the campaign focuses on the illnesses not the drugs. It will be interesting to see public reaction to this.

BA: So let's have a look at the second company. This company is a cable operator. Well, it provides cable television to thousands and thousands of homes but it wants to expand and it's developing a new high-speed Internet service. Now,

this service uses cables not phone wires and this means it is very fast, 100 times faster than a normal phone line. As you know, the number of people who are using the internet is growing and growing and everyone wants instant information so this is a company with a great future.

2.5 Listening

TA = Tom Armstrong
RH = Rachel Humphries
RH: So Tom, what do you know about the Virgin Group?
TA: They're a very large group, erm, they exist in a lot of different sectors and they're run by Richard Branson - they're British.
RH: Yes, yeah and they, erm they produce, er Virgin Cola, don't they?
TA: Yeah and I think they're also famous for the airline, the Virgin Atlantic.
RH: Um, and er they have a radio station – Virgin radio.
TA: Yeah, and they still have the megastores, and I think they have megastores all over the world now,
RH: Yes,
TA: selling videos, music. What do you know about Benetton?
RH: Well, they're Italian, and they're very successful clothing manufacturers.
TA: I think they produce sportswear now.
RH: Yes, that's right – sportswear, and erm, another, they have another trademark called Sisley, which produces more expensive clothing.
TA: And Mercedes-Benz – do you know anything about them?
RH: Well they manufacture expensive, luxury cars erm and they're, erm German I think, or maybe German – American now, perhaps.
TA: I think they're part of the Daimler Chrysler Group, which again is a large group ... I've heard that they also produce a very small car called the Smart,
RH: Oh right, it's good for the towns and cities,
TA: Yeah.

RH: And what about Sony?
TA: Oh Sony, they're, they're as far as I know they're still the world leaders in electronics, and produce, for example, the Sony Walkman.
RH: Mmm, and they're Japanese.
TA: Yeah.
RH: And er, what else do they produce? ... computer games
TA: Yeah, and they also do music now; they did the music for the film the *Titanic*.

2.6 Business Communication

Speaker: A lot of you will have heard of this next multinational's products, but I suspect that fewer of you will have heard of the company itself; LVMH.
First of all, what does LVMH stand for? The answer is the world's leading luxury goods group. Louis Vuitton Moët Hennessy.
So what does the group do? Well, of course, it specialises in luxury products ..., and it operates in a number of sectors. As you can see from the chart, these are wines and spirits, fashion and leather goods, fragrances and cosmetics and selective retailing. Look at the brand names in each sector. Each sector includes world-famous names.
Let's look first at wines and spirits. LVMH is the world leader in champagne production with brands such as Dom Pérignon, Moët and Chandon and Pommery.

UNIT 3 *Travel*

3.2 Language Focus

MS = Mike Smith PG = Pam García
MS: Hello Pam. It's Mike, how are you?
PG: Oh hello Mike, I'm fine thanks, and you?
MS: Oh, not too bad. Could I speak to Rosalind Harrison?
PG: Oh, I'm sorry, Mike. I'm afraid she's out of the office at the moment – she's visiting a client in Manchester.
MS: Oh, OK. Well, maybe you can help. It's about the sales conference, is she coming over to

Warsaw next Tuesday?

PG: Yes, she's flying out on Monday morning, but she's visiting the Gdansk office first.

MS: So when is she coming to Warsaw then?

PG: I'm not sure, possibly on Tuesday, or she may spend another day in Gdansk and then go to Warsaw on Wednesday.

MS: OK, well I'm having a meeting with our Marketing Manager on Wednesday morning. That's at nine thirty. She's welcome to join in on that, and then I really must see her some time on Wednesday about the product launch.

PG: OK, I'll let her know.

MS: Thanks Pam. Hey, are you coming over with Rosalind?

PG: No, I'm not this time, but I am coming over in September!

MS: That's great, I'll look forward to seeing you! Bye for now!

PG: Bye.

3.5 Listening

Int = Interviewer

CK = Colin Knapp

Int: Colin, do you travel on business very often?

CK: I travel to Thailand about two to three times per year.

Int: And how long is the flight from England to Thailand?

CK: The flight is about twelve hours.

Int: Uh, huh. Do you enjoy that long flight?

CK: It's, it is OK as long as I take plenty of reading, and they normally have three to four films.

Int: And do you watch all the films?

CK: I watch all of the films because I find it very difficult to sleep on a, on a plane.

Int: OK. Do you erm suffer from jet lag after the flight?

CK: Er, I suffer jet lag, erm in Thailand it lasts for about one, one day.

Int: Uh, hu; and when you return to England?

CK: It is worse, for some reason, and is about three days.

Int: So travelling back to England is, is less pleasant?

CK: It is less pleasant, but that apparently is quite common.

Int: OK. Erm, and what's the reason for your visits to Thailand?

CK: It's to teach and to do some business with the University.

Int: Why do you travel to Thailand to do business? Why can't you do that by telephone or fax?

CK: Because our discussions are quite complex and it w..., it is too complex for telephone and fax.

Int: OK. When you visit Thailand do you experience a culture gap?

CK: There is a culture gap, yes.

Int: Erm, and what are the ... can you give me any examples of that?

CK: They are very polite people, and so there are times when you may think they agree with you, but they are, they say 'yes' because they think it is polite.

Int: OK. So the, the way people communicate is different?

CK: They communicate in a different way, yes.

Int: OK. And so can you give people visiting Thailand any tips, for their visit?

CK: Erm, always try to be polite, and be respectful, and on first meeting try not to look the person in the eye, erm too often.

Business Communication

3.6 INTRODUCTIONS AND GREETINGS

1 **W:** I'd like to introduce you to Señor Iglesias.
Señor Iglesias this is Duncan Grove.
DG: Pleased to meet you.
SI: How do you do.

2 **M:** Do you know Caroline Courtney?
David: No, hello.
David: Pleased to meet you. I'm David Walker.
Caroline: Nice to meet you.

3 **SB:** Hello, Ms Barty?
AB: Yes.
SB: I'm Stephen Brown.
AB: Oh, yes, hello. Nice to meet you. You work with Roslyn Davis, don't you?

SB: Yes, that's right.

4 **M:** Sofia, this is Barry. Barry, Sofia.
S: Hello, Barry. Nice to meet you.
B: Hello. Pleased to meet you.

5 **M:** Let me introduce Miss Kim. Miss Kim, this is Mr Kinzett.
Mr Kinzett: Pleased to meet you.
Miss Kim: Pleased to meet you.

6 **K:** Hi, I'm John.
F: Hello, my name's Fiona.

3.7 SOCIALISING

Colin: Hello, how are you?

Michelle: I'm fine thanks . How are you?

Colin: Fine. It's nice to see you.

Michelle: You too.

Colin: Can I get you a drink?

Michelle: Oh, yes thank you. I'll have a glass of wine please.

Colin: Red or white?

Michelle: White please.

Colin: I'm afraid there's only red.

Michelle: Oh, that's all right. Red's fine.

Colin: (He spills a little of the drink) Oh, I'm so sorry!

Michelle: That's all right, don't worry about it.

Colin: I'm terribly sorry.

Michelle: Really, it doesn't matter.

3.8 Roger: Hello, Colin. Just to say the taxi will be here in a few minutes.

Colin: Oh, Roger, let me introduce you to Michelle.

Roger: Hello, Michelle. Nice to meet you.

Michelle: Pleased to meet you. Sorry, I didn't catch your name.

Roger: I'm Roger.

Colin: We're having dinner at The Lemon Tree. Would you like to join us?

Michelle: That's very kind of you. I'd love to, but I'm afraid I have to get home. My parents are coming to stay this weekend.

Colin: Can we give you a lift?

Michelle: Oh, that would be great. Thank you very much. I'll just get my coat.

3.9 Michelle: Thanks very much for the lift.
Colin: Pleasure. Don't mention it.
Michelle: Bye. Have a nice meal.
Roger: Thanks very much. Have a good weekend.

Unit 4 *Troubleshooting*

4.2 Language Focus

AB = Anna Brook
BW = Belinda Waters
AB: I don't think car manufacturers and car dealers think about female customers at all.
BW: I know what you mean. Car dealers don't seem to listen to what women say they want.
AB: Yes, they should take us seriously. After all women are buying more cars these days.
BW: Yes, so they should have more women selling cars.
AB: Mm. The dealers are nearly always men and they do such a hard sell. I think they ought to use a soft-sell approach.
BW: I agree. I really don't like the hard sell. You know, I also think that things like children's car seats and car phones should be available as standard.
AB: Yes definitely, why don't they fit car phones in all new cars? Women on their own feel much safer with a phone in the car.
BW: And they should change the adverts too, I think.
AB: Yes, I think there should be lots of product information in adverts. They ought to tell us about things like petrol consumption and safety features.
BW: I hate these adverts just showing us fast cars in exotic locations.
AB: Me too.

4.5 Listening

Int = Interviewer   M = Manager
Int: Why do you think troubleshooting, or solving problems, is so important in business?
M: Well these days, erm, business is extremely competitive and it's competitive in terms of time and in terms of money. Whenever a company tries to compete with another company, it tries to get a new product out quickly and it tries to do it without spending too much money. Problems, when they arise, cost money and they waste time.
Int: And, are there any particular areas which are typical trouble spots?
M: Starting at the very beginning of a project, quite often people don't plan effectively. You can never plan early enough, especially in a large and complex project. Part of that planning involves making sure that everybody on the project understands his or her role; and that the objectives of the project are regularly reviewed, so that everybody understands how the project is going to meet the needs of the market, and whether it is still relevant.
Int: And do you think that, erm everyone has a role in troubleshooting and anticipating problems, or do you see it as only a managerial skill?
M: I think it can quite often happen that managers start a project, think it's going very well, walk away from it and then are very surprised six months later when it's going wrong. Er, everybody, at whatever level, should make sure that they ask the right questions, and indeed try to, as you say, anticipate problems and raise those problems with their managers and with their colleagues at regular review intervals.
Int: Do you have any other tips for solving problems?
M: It's very important that a project team communicates well within itself and also to people outside the team. You should try to have a democratic spirit in a project, allowing people to speak openly, to ask questions and to feel that they own the project as much as the managers or the client may do.
Int: What's the one most important strategy to avoid problems?
M: In my opinion, in order to avoid problems happening you should be realistic. You should be realistic in the number of people working on the project, the cost of the project and the size of the project. When you put pressure on a project because you don't have enough people working on it, or you are spending too much money, you create problems. Pressure means problems, so to avoid problems, reduce the pressure.

UNIT 5
Company History

5.2 Lead-in

In 1894 Michael Marks and Tom Spencer formed a partnership.
In 1928 they registered the *St Michael* trademark.
In 1930 the company opened the Marble Arch store on Oxford Street in London.
In 1931 they introduced canned goods such as tomato soup.
In 1975 Marks and Spencer opened stores in Paris and Brussels.
In 1988 they opened two stores in Hong Kong.
In 1997 they won the Queen's award for Export Achievement for the fifth time.

5.5 Language Practice

Int = Interviewer
FW = Faith Walker
Int: When did you buy your first pair of Doc Martens?
FW: When I was 24 – that was in 1987.
Int: How much did they cost then?
FW: Erm, at that time they cost £25.00.
Int: Where did you buy them?
FW: I bought them in London, in Oxford Street.
Int: What colour were they?
FW: They were cherry red.
Int: Why did you choose Doc Martens?
FW: Well, because they were very fashionable in the 80s and I liked the style.
Int: Do you still wear Doc Martens?

FW: Yes, I still like the style.

5.6 Listening

5.6a Pat Woodgate: Hello. I'm going to talk to you today about the key developments in the history of the company I work for and then tell you about the company's current position.

I am based in the Loss Control Department of Zurich Municipal which is part of the Zurich Financial Services Group. Zurich Municipal is a strategic business unit dealing solely with the public sector, e.g. local government, national health trusts, etc.

The company began its history when Zurich Insurance Company was founded 125 years ago in Zurich, Switzerland under the name of Versicherungs-Verein, or Insurance Association.

5.6b They started business in May 1873, initially providing re-insurance – that is where they provide insurance cover to other insurance companies so that the risk is distributed throughout the market. They quickly entered into the field of accident insurances and obtained licences to conduct business in other European countries in 1875.

In 1922 the Zurich Insurance Company opened for business in the UK, with London-based headquarters. After many years of increased growth, in 1993 they took over the business of Municipal Mutual Insurance, who were the previous market leaders in providing insurance to the public sector.

In September 1998 the Zurich Insurance Company merged with British American Financial Services, that is the financial services operation of British American Tobacco Industries, thus forming Zurich Financial Services Group.

The group now has over 68,000 employees and over 30 million customers in over 50 countries. It is one of the ten largest companies world-wide, offering insurance and asset management.

Unit 6 *Retailing*

6.3 Listening

Int = Interviewer
SR = Sarah Rochford
Int: How often do you visit an IKEA store?
SR: I probably visit the store about twice a year. I keep the erm catalogue at home and look through that during the year, and then make a visit about twice a year.
Int: What do you think of their products?
SR: I think they have a very good range of products, erm I'm impressed with the quality of them; you get good quality for the price that you pay, and additionally I think that most of the products are environmentally sound.
Int: How about the stores - do you like them?
SR: Well, it's nice to try out the products, to be able to see them and try them out, and the layout of the store is very nice, erm they do have a good selection of household accessories in the Marketplace erm and it's very easy for people with children – they have a playroom and pushchairs and suchlike.
Int: What type of things do you buy at IKEA?
SR: Well, I usually buy functional items such as bookcases and lamps and things like that, and then sometimes I buy textiles and bed linen.
Int: Are there any aspects of shopping at IKEA that you don't like?
SR: Oh there are! erm it can be very crowded because it's a popular store, you can get a lot of people. This results often in very long queues at the checkouts; you can wait for quite a long time to pay for your goods, so that's my main problem with shopping there.
Int: So are you planning another trip to IKEA?
SR: Yes, I expect so. I'll probably go again in January for the sales.

6.4 Language Focus Two

1 I prefer sales assistants who let me look round by myself.
2 I think it's important to have packaging that clearly shows the ingredients.
3 Because of the children I need shops which have car parks.
4 I like shops that offer a wide variety of goods.
5 I like shopping malls where all my favourite shops are in one place.
6 I don't like door-to-door sales people who put you under pressure and try to sell you things you don't want.

Business Communication

6.5 Through the switchboard

Conversation 1
A: Good morning, Dunton Associates.
B: Oh hello, could I speak to Amanda Holt, please?
A: Just one moment.
I'm afraid Ms Holt's line is busy.
B: Could you put me through to her secretary?
A: Just one moment. I'm afraid that line is busy, too. I can put you through to the message desk, if you like.
B: No thanks, I'll call back later.
A: Thank you. Goodbye.

Conversation 2
A: Smith, Thomas & Manton.
B: Could you put me through to Barry Smith, please?
A: It's ringing for you.
C: Hello, Barry Smith speaking.
B: Hello Mr Smith, it's Melanie Grant here.
C: Hello, Ms Grant.

6.6 Direct Line

Conversation 1
A: Hello, Joanna Coutts. How may I help you?
B: Hello. This is Chris Parry. Could I speak to Pat Summers, please?
A: I'm afraid she's out of the office at the moment. Can I get her to call

you?
B: Yes, please.
A: Can you give me your number?
B: 03071 888935.
And, I'm sorry, your name again?
B: Chris Parry.
A: OK Ms Parry, I'll ask her to call you.
B: Thank you.
A: Thank you. Goodbye.
B: Goodbye.

Conversation 2
A: Hello, Pat Summers.
B: Oh, hello Pat. It's Chris Parry here.
A: Hello, Chris. How are you?
B: Fine thanks ...

Unit 7 *Products*

7.2 Lead-in

Salesperson: We are proud to present this important new addition to our range. It comes with active speakers and its great new colours are stylish and fashionable. As well as the speakers, we offer you all the features you normally expect – this hi-spec product has a 22-track programmable memory, random play and more. We think you'll find £79.99 is an amazing price, and we're sure you'll be keen to order your personal player right away.

7.6 Listening

Int = Interviewer
VA = Verena Adams
Int: Verena, how important is advertising in selling products?
VA: Well, it's an important marketing tool, and it works in a number of different ways.
Int: What are some of the ways it can work?
VA: Advertising can inform or persuade or remind or motivate; obviously the type of ad depends on the product.
Int: Oh, I see, but could you give us an example?
VA: Well, erm, for example – a low cost, erm low cost fast moving consumer goods, erm like chocolate bars or soft drinks, erm are going to be advertised differently from consumer durables like televisions or washing machines. You'd advertise Tango differently from the way you'd advertise a car.
Int: Right, so how would a Tango advertisement work?
VA: Well, Tango's a fizzy drink, an orange fizzy drink in a can, erm, so it's aimed at the teenage market. You'd go for eye-catching, attention-getting advertising; you'd try to create a modern brand image.
Int: Uh, hu
VA: Erm, television ads which were created, erm, had a very crazy, funny, colourful campaign, erm aimed to motivate the teenage market to buy; and they were very successful.
Int: I see. How about advertising a car?
VA: Well for a car you're into a different product sector, erm, and a different target audience. You're trying to persuade that market to spend a lot of money, so you'd go for press ads, with lots of copy – details of the models and the prices and the features and all that kind of thing – and you'd probably back it up with a television campaign to show the cars in action.
Int: Who decides, then, who actually decides which sort of media to use?
VA: Erm, well, advertisers go for different mixes of media, erm but basically it's the advertising agency who makes the choices; the agency is the link between the manufacturer of the product and the public, and erm, they create a brief of the different, of the most suc... most useful kinds of media to use.
Int: What do you think makes a good advertisement, then?
VA: In my opinion, a good advertisement always concentrates on the product.

7.7 Business Communication

Do you have friends and family you would like to see more often? When you phone colleagues would you like to see their faces? The ViaTV Desktop videophone means that you can!
As you can see it's small and elegant and ideal for the office or for the home or for business trips.
It's very easy to set up. All you need is a touch-tone phone. You don't need a computer and you don't need any special software. It's also very easy to use; it's as easy as making a normal telephone call.
The ViaTV Desktop video phone has many features. Firstly, it has full-colour motion video which means you can see the other person's gestures and changes of expression. The picture quality is excellent and the adjustable picture setting means you can change to 'sharp' mode to get a fantastically clear image. This, of course, is just ideal for viewing designs or documents. The audio quality is exactly the same as a normal telephone call.
In addition, the Via Desktop Video phone also has a preview mode so that you can check what you look like before the other person sees you! And finally, the privacy mode is an important feature. You can use it to block the image but keep voice connection.
Now, of course, just as with any means of communication, fax machines or e-mail for example, each party needs to have a set. We have a special offer on at the moment, so now is the time to buy the ViaTV Desktop phone. Put yourself in the picture.

Unit 8 *People*

8.2 Language Focus One

PT = Philippa Taylor
DG = Dan Goldman
PT: Right, Dan. You know that the aim of this performance appraisal is to look at how you're doing and to identify any areas where you need to make some changes.
So, what's your assessment? How are you getting on?
DG: Pretty good, I guess. I'm really

enjoying the work here.

PT: That's good to hear. Is there anything you're particularly pleased with?

DG: Erm, yeah. I was very pleased with the way things went on the Silverton project. It was a great team – really motivating to work with them, and to learn from them.

PT: Good, yes, I think you worked really well on that project ....

PT: OK. So now are there any aspects of the job where you think there is room for improvement?

DG: Well I'm still having some difficulties with my time management.

PT: Why do you think that is?

DG: I guess I'm a bit too optimistic about how much I can do in a day! But I really do want to get better at organising my time.

PT: OK. So what are you going to do about that?

DG: Well, I'm going to try to prioritise more, to deal with the things that are really important. I'm also going to set myself more realistic deadlines.

PT: Good, OK, that sounds sensible.

DG: And, I've finally got a place on a time management course and I'm doing that next month.

PT: Excellent. Who's running it this time?

DG: It's Scott Henman.

PT: Oh, he's good. I think that will be very useful.

8.5 Listening

Int = Interviewer
ML = Morna Lawson

Int: Can you tell me what gives you satisfaction in your job?

ML: Well, there's different things really, er obviously salary is important, status is important – I want to be respected for what I do – erm but most importantly I can't bear being bored, with routines, so I want the freedom to develop my role really.

Int: So it's important your manager gives you autonomy.

ML: Yes.

Int: What management style do you respond well to?

ML: Well, I like them, really I like my manager to be fairly hands-off, yet available, so I'm allowed to do what, I'm allowed to get on with it and the manager is there to support me.

Int: OK. I know you've worked in Spain and Britain. Are there any differences between the workplace culture in the two countries?

ML: Mmm, it was a while, a few years ago that I was in Spain, and I think that Britain and Spain have probably become more similar, but the thing I noticed most was that the Spanish work in order to enjoy their lives far more so than they do in Britain.

Int: Right, Could you describe your best manager?

ML: Erm, a woman I worked with in Spain, who enjoyed her job, enjoyed life; we had a good time at work, erm, and most of all she allowed me to get on with it, make my mistakes – it wasn't the end of the world, and I learnt a lot from it.

8.6 Business Communication

Int = Interviewer
LC = Lisa Crawford

Int: What do you do?

LC: I work in the travel industry. I'm a tour representative for Sun Travel.

Int: That sounds fun. What does the job involve?

LC: Well it's not all sun and sea. In fact it's often very hard work. Basically, it involves looking after people when they're on holiday. I'm responsible for sorting out any problems and I often have to deal with complaints. The work also involves entertaining the holidaymakers and their children.

Int: It sounds like hard work. But what about the perks?

LC: Well the obvious one is that you get to travel a lot and experience different cultures. I really value that aspect of the work.

Int: What about your colleagues? Are they mainly men or women?

LC: In the company I work for there are more women than men, but I'm not sure that that's true of the industry as a whole.

8.7 SD = Sam Davis

SD: I'm responsible for recruiting people to jobs. I often have to deal with the complaints and problems of people working in the company. The work also often involves training people. Most of my colleagues are women, but the mix in the company as a whole is about 50-50.

Unit 9
Business Environment

9.2 Language Focus 1

1 The average wage may be quite low in Caracas or a Big Mac might cost a lot there.

2 It takes a long time to earn enough to buy a Big Mac in Lagos. There may be a luxury tax on it in Nigeria.

3 In Chicago the competition from other hamburger companies could affect the price.

4 I could be wrong, but I think the Big Mac and a portion of fries costs about £3.00 in London.

5 Big Macs may cost more to produce in Lagos, but it can't be because of the cost of labour. Labour costs are so low there.

6 Perhaps Big Macs are more expensive in Britain because demand is high.

7 Salaries are probably higher in Frankfurt than in London.

9.4 Language Practice

BA = Business analyst

BA: OK Let's start with some news about IKEA. The Swedish furniture giant [IKEA] has continued to do excellent business this year. IKEA has a global presence with stores in around 30 countries and it is continuing to expand, opening new stores every year. Its biggest market is Europe with sales accounting for 84.4% of total sales. Within Europe, Scandinavia, Germany, France and the UK are very significant markets. Of these Germany is the largest, with France, Scandinavia and the UK having almost equal shares. North America accounts for 14.4 % of sales and Asia for 1.2%

IKEA's products are designed and developed in Sweden by IKEA Sweden, but manufactured all over the world. IKEA has suppliers in 65 countries. 19.2% of the suppliers are in the Far East and 17.2% in East Central Europe. Just 3.3% are in North America. IKEA's success depends on these local suppliers, so before opening a store in a new market, IKEA establishes a link with a supplier in that market. It chooses carefully; criteria for selecting suppliers may include proximity to raw materials, reliable access to distribution channels and low-costs.....

9.5 Listening

TA = Tom Armstrong

TA: I'm going to talk about the world's most competitive countries, and to do this we are using an index, where we can see that the United States of America is at the top of the index, and the questions we must ask are 'why are some countries higher than others?' America is at the top of the index because of continuous economic growth. We note that the Netherlands is Europe's highest competitor, or best competitor, in fourth position, and this again is because of a successful economic restructuring.

Singapore comes in the second position, at number two – it is the most technologically advanced economy in the world.

Perhaps surprisingly Germany is below countries such as Canada and Britain, and is in 14th place, as a result of a re-unification process which is very, very expensive. Brazil is equivalent to Greece and the Czech Republic in having problems with infrastructure, and finds itself in 37th position.

9.7

1 We increase sales every year.
2 We need an increase in sales.
3 We want to decrease the costs.
4 They won't accept a decrease in their salaries.
5 Exports cost too much.
6 We hope to increase exports.
7 We need to decrease imports.
8 We import and export.

9.7 Business Communication

1 Sales increased slightly from 1991 to 1992.
2 Sales decreased dramatically from 1992 to 1993.
3 In 1993 sales improved significantly.
4 Sales rose from 1993 to 1994.
5 Sales grew steadily from 1994 to 1997.
6 Sales fell sharply from 1999 to 2000.

Unit 10 *Finance*

10.3 Language Practice One

CARDINAL NUMBERS

In 1999 The minimum wage was set at £3.60 an hour for adults and £3.00 for young workers aged between eighteen and twenty-one. Surveys showed that most employers wanted the minimum wage to be £3.50, but at least they are pleased the government did not set it at £4.00 as many workers demanded.

10.4 ORDINAL NUMBERS

The most expensive place to live in Europe is Oslo. In the world ranking it comes in fifth position. Paris is another expensive city and comes in at seventh place in the world ranking. London is in tenth place – a dramatic move from the previous year when it was in twenty – eighth place. Surprisingly, Stockholm is cheaper than London and comes in at thirteenth position. Dusseldorf and Lyon both come lower down at twenty-first position and Frankfurt is in twenty-sixth place.

10.5 DECIMALS

Annual holidays vary greatly from country to country. The Spanish take an average of 32.1 days holiday per year compared with the Hungarians and the Britsh who have only 22.1 days – just over four working weeks. In the Czech republic, annual holidays are even less generous, with the average number of days at just 19.5.

10.6 PERCENTAGES

RA = Robyn Alton
MM: = Matthew Mead

RA: It surprises me that people spend 22% of their income on food and drink. I spend approximately 10% of my income, erm on food and drink in a year.

MM: uh hu. I spend about 14%, I'd say, so a bit more than you, but er, less than the pie chart. It seems a lot, doesn't it?

RA: It seems a lot. What about housing?

MM: Housing; I spend about 27%, erm which is quite a lot, it's a lot of my income, er for one area, but I'm buying a second house, so it costs more money. Transport seemed quite high, I thought, er 15.7% for transport. I spend only about 6 or 7%. What about you?

RA: I spend 15% erm of my total income on transportation, er so that didn't surprise me, that figure. What about household goods and services?

MM: Well, I've only got 4%, but erm, I'm not doing much work on my house at the moment, so it's, it's not a great deal of my income. What about you?

RA: I spend 12% on household goods and services; I spend erm money on decorating, gardening erm so that's, that's a large part of my expenditure.

MM: Right. I spend about 16% – 15 or 16% on leisure goods and services, so about the same as the pie chart.

RA: That's similar to me. I spend about 15%.

MM: Right. That's on going to the

gym, sports, maybe some travel.

RA: That's, that's very similar for me. What about tobacco? I've, I, I spend 0% on tobacco.

MM: Mmm. I don't smoke, so it's not an important part for me, and er 2% seems very high.

RA: It seems high to me too.

10.7c Pronunciation

1 Each year interest rates rise.
2 Last year interest rates rose.
3 We'll raise our prices by 2% in April.
4 The bank raised our overdraft.
5 I hope this situation doesn't arise again.
6 The problem arose because the machine wasn't working properly.

Listening

10.8 Int = Interviewer
KJ = Keith Jackson

Int: Keith, can you explain what a profit and loss account is, and the main purpose of it?

KJ: Right, well, basically it's a statement of the cash available to a company, the money available to a company, to erm, continue its operations. Erm, and it's information to managers in helping them make their decisions in running the company, and very importantly, it's information to the shareholders who are the owners of a public company – it tells shareholders how well the company is performing and how well their investment in that company is working for them.

Int: Right, so looking at this particular profit and loss account erm, which figures would managers be most interested in?

KJ: OK, well, turnover, for example, the first there, this should show managers the total sum of money which is coming into the company, and reading from right to left managers can see whether the company is in fact generating more or less cash year on year. Erm, now turnover is not the same as profit, of course, because it actually costs money to produce, or to run the company; so second down from turnover we look at operating profit erm, this will show what surplus, or how much money the company's making after paying for its production costs. So looking at the operating profit this should give managers the idea on how efficiently they're running the company, for example.

Int: Right, and erm you mentioned the shareholders. Which figures are they most interested in?

KJ: Well, looking at the example here, they, their eyes would probably go straight to the bottom line – we have the earnings per share – they would like to see how much they are earning on their investment, so the money they put into the company in the form of shares, they want to know whether they are earning more money from the company's operations. And we can see here that their earnings per share – so the money they earn on each pound they put into the company – is increasing.

Unit 11 *Corporate Responsibility*

11.2 Language Focus One

CH = CleanHome Manager
MC = Management Consultant

CH: What'll happen if our profits fall?

MC: If your profits fall the shareholders dividend will decrease.

CH: If our shareholders' dividend decreases they'll be very unhappy.

MC: Yes, your situation might be very serious if the public loses confidence in the company.

CH: Our share price might fall if people lose confidence. I think we should consider this matter seriously.

11.3 Language Practice One

1 If a company conducts irresponsible marketing, customers won't buy their products.
2 Small companies will go out of business if their customers don't pay on time.
3 Many customers won't buy products if companies test them on animals.
4 If a multinational company pays 'first world' prices for goods from developing countries, those suppliers will become self-sufficient.
5 If a company delays payments, what will the consequences be?

11.4 Listening

Int: Kevin, can I ask you – do you think big business behaves responsibly?

KM: Erm, the simple answer is no, no I don't think it behaves responsibly, erm I think that it's not the job of a business to behave responsibly, it's the job of a business to make money, and I think they always put making money as their top priority before the effects of what, of, of their actions on people and environment.

Int: Can you give me some examples of, of how they don't think about people and the environment?

KM: Certainly. Erm, for example factory farming is very bad for the environment, but it makes erm factory farming companies very high profits; erm companies aren't concerned about the destruction of the rain forest and they're often not concerned about the conditions their workers work in.

Int: Erm, thinking about that then; are there any products that you don't buy?

KM: Well I, I never buy meat that I know comes from a factory farm; erm I never buy clothing that I know's been made in a sweatshop or with child labour; erm I always try not to buy products that have been tested on animals – I check the labels in the shop to make sure they haven't been tested on animals, and I never buy anything from a company that I know invests heavily in a country where the government abuses human rights of the people who live there.

Int: OK. Well, looking at the other side of the coin, are there any products that you do try to buy?

KM: Well, I, I always try to buy erm cleaning things, you know like washing up liquid, that I know contain very low levels of phosphates, because phosphates kill fish in rivers; erm I usually buy Traidcraft coffee, erm it's from Oxfam and it helps people in developing countries, and I always buy free-range eggs – they taste nicer as well.

Unit 12 *Competition*

12.3 Listening

Int = Interviewer
KJ = Keith Jackson

12.3a Int: The global market place is very competitive; how can a company become a market leader?

KJ: Well I think basically by having a good product and using good marketing. But to become a market leader there are three main strategies, I think – cost, so reducing cost, producing more cheaply, selling more cheaply; er differentiation – that is making your products appear very special in the market place, and innovation – so finding new products and new ways to market products, which is particularly important in the, as you said, the global market.

12.3b Int: Can we take a concrete example and look at the soft drinks market? Can you explain how these three factors work?

KJ: Fine, well if you look at erm, cost as focus, or a cost-focus strategy, erm let's take cola for example, erm we know that big supermarket chains in the UK – Safeways or Tescos or Sainsbury's – they produce their own cola at low cost and can sell it more cheaply than Coca-Cola, for example. Erm differentiation, I mean, a good example is, I think, Tango; they've managed to penetrate the market and be competitive by using a very

interesting and rather wacky advertising campaign for their product. Erm, and innovation, for example, Virgin we know of as er a music or airline company; they also own cinemas, and through the cinemas, the distribution channel of their cinemas, they've managed now to promote their own version of cola, so they've ... innovation in controlling distribution means they can be competitive in the cola market, for example.

12.3c Int: Keith, you mentioned erm, some very famous names there, erm, companies which compete in the global market place. Are there any particular problems faced by companies who, who wish to be competitive in a global market?

KJ: Well yes there are. I mentioned Virgin and Coca-Cola for example, these are global players in the soft drinks market, erm they do face particular problems. We could take another example – McDonald's in the food retail business. For example McDonald's, the main part of their selling strategy is the quality of their products, the standardised quality. It's very difficult for a company to control or guarantee the quality of their product on a global scale. Erm particularly where they have to be sensitive to or adapt to local cultures and customer expectations. A good example with regard to McDonald's is the fact that they do not sell beef burgers, so burgers made of beef, in India, for example, because that would possibly offend local cultures there. Of course globally marketing becomes a particular problem – can companies erm communicate the same or a similar standardised message about their product in different language regions of the world? And McDonald's we know are very lucky in this respect because they have a good product in the sense that the product they offer is recognised among a large population, youthful population of the world as symbolising the

American lifestyle, for example, so McDonald's are very lucky in the power of the product and the message they have on a global scale. Other companies of course have much greater difficulties with their products.

12.5 Business Communication

Int: So Brett. What do you think your strengths are?

Brett: Well, I enjoy working with people as part of a team. I think the best results come from working together. I've found that's true in all the projects I've worked on.

Int: Well, Barry. You seem to have done lots of different things. How have you found the time for them all?

Barry: I am just very active. I try to organise my studies and my other interests so I can do as many things as possible. I think it's good to meet lots of different people and have lots of different experiences.

Int: Why do you want to work in this area?

Julie: I think marketing's a really interesting area. I've really enjoyed doing my marketing course and it's convinced me that this is the right area.

Pearson Education Limited
Edinburgh Gate
Harlow
Essex CM20 2JE
England
and Associated Companies throughout the World.

First Published in 2000

Set in ITC Stone Serif and ITC Stone Sans

Printed in Spain by Gráficas Estella

ISBN 0582 334543

Illustrations
Illustrated by Andy Baker (Debut Art), Matt Buckley, Ian Dicks (illustrators.co), George Foster, Tim Kahane, Bernice Lum (illustrators.co), Carol Morley (Thorogood Illustration), Sandy Nicholls (Three in a Box inc.) and Gavin Reece (New Division).

Cover illustration by Sarah Jones (Debut Art)

Acknowledgements
I would like to thank the many colleagues who commented on earlier drafts of the material and helped shape it into its current form. Special thanks to Kevin Manton for valuable comments on the Students' Book and for creating interesting tasks for the Workbook; to Verena Adams for staunch support and knowledgeable input on the advertising industry; to those colleagues who gave freely of their time to make recordings, especially Tom Armstrong, Rachel Humphries, Keith Jackson, Colin Knapp, Morna Lawson, Howard Middle and Pat Woodgate; and to Linda Davey for her help compiling the Teacher's notes. I am indebted to my editor, Judith Walters, for her tremendous input editing the manuscript and preparing it for publication.

The author and publisher would like to thank the following people:

Bernie Hayden, Rosi Jillett and Hester Lott.

We would especially like to thank Alicja Kalinska, Janusz Szczygiel, Ana Garcia de Oteiza, Erica Hall, Margaret Cobb, Marilyn Moylan, Jeremy Townend and Colleen Cheney for reporting on the material.

We would also like to thank:

Robyn Alton, Ann Hislop, Bruce Neal and Stephen Nicholl.

We are grateful to the following for permission to reproduce copyright material:

Cafedirect® for an extract from a CAFEDIRECT® Advertisement (info@cafedirect.co.uk); Consumers Association/Which? Ltd for adapted extracts from 'Internet Shopping protection needed' in WHICH? magazine, September 1997. Which? is a monthly independent consumer magazine published by Consumers' Association, 2 Marylebone Road, London NW1 4DF; Dyson Appliances Ltd for an extract from DOING A DYSON (1996); Edizione Holding for extracts from their GROUP PROFILE AND FINANCIAL HIGHLIGHTS 31.12.97; Express Newspapers plc for adapted extracts from 'Check-ins yes, cheque-outs no' in THE EXPRESS 12.4.94. 'Car Giant Sends in the Spy Girls' by David Benson in THE EXPRESS 9.12.93. 'Big Firms "Cheat" with late payment' by Sally Hamilton in THE EXPRESS 12.9.94; Financial Times Ltd for an extract from 'Pearson Information Division' in GET 98, YOUR ULTIMATE CAREER GUIDE; First Direct for text from 'First Direct' information leaflet – C/15,1997 Developed by FD Com. First Direct's communications forum; Granada TV for extracts from a job advertisement in THE GUARDIAN, 20.7.98; Guardian Newspapers Ltd for adapted extracts from 'Use: Design and Function in the 20th Century' in THE GUARDIAN (date unknown) 'Use: Design and Function in the 20th Century' in THE GUARDIAN (date unknown), 'Chocs Away' in THE GUARDIAN 19.11.94. 'Inventor scores a first as Britain cleans up in Europe' by Kamal Ahmed in THE GUARDIAN 1.2.97. 'Factors considered when choosing that first job' in THE GUARDIAN 10.10.98. 'Barcodes, Bars & Stripes' by Iqbal Hussain in THE GUARDIAN EDUCATION 6.9.94; the author, Ian Harding for an adapted extract from his article 'Bic's Success in a Throwaway World' in THE EUROPEAN 16-22.9.94; Haymarket Management Publications Ltd for an adapted extract from 'Name, shame & claim from UK's late payers' in MANAGEMENT TODAY July 1998; Independent Newspapers UK Ltd for adapted extracts from the articles 'UK fifth in cost of groceries league' by Patrick Hosking in THE INDEPENDENT 8.12.92. 'Made in Japan, Sold on Britain' by David Bowen in INDEPENDENT ON SUNDAY 15 August 1993. 'Does Gender make the Manager?' by Cristina Stuart in THE INDEPENDENT ON SUNDAY 8.5.94; Inland Reveue for job advert taken from THE GUARDIAN October 1998; Innovations (Mail Order) Plc for adapted extracts from INNOVATIONS CATALOGUE; Kwik-Fit Holdings plc for text from their advertisement 'You can't get better than a Kwik-Fit fitter!'; Lindt and Sprungli (UK) Ltd for text - list of ingredients from Lindt chocolate wrapper; the author, Jane Mulvagh for an adapted extract from her article 'The ABC of DMs' in THE EUROPEAN 2–5.9.93; Jonathan Phang /BBC Worldwide for adapted extracts from BBC Website http://www.bbc.co.uk/education/trouble/models.htm A MODEL MD; Reuters Ltd for extract from an advertisement in *THE GUARDIAN* 7.9.98; Solo Syndication Ltd for a slightly adapted extract from 'No quick respite in sight for M & S' by Joanne Hart in THE EVENING

STANDARD; Time Life Syndication for an extract from 'Afizz with competition' by Barbara Rudolph in *TIME MAGAZINE* 19.6.93; Traidcraft, Gateshead – UK for an extract from a Recruitment Advertisement; University of Manchester & UMIST Careers Service for adapted extracts from UMIST Careers Service web site – http://www.man.ac.uk/careers/students/apps/CV-basics.html.

We have been unable to trace the copyright holders of the *MSL* Advertisement, 'Home is where the expenses rack up' by Harriot Lane Fox, or *VIATV VIDEOPHONES*, and would appreciate any information which would enable us to do so.

Photo Acknowledgments
We are grateful to the following for permission to reproduce copyright photographs:

Asda/I.S.I: 138(TL); BIC: 51(whole page), 55(C); Britvic Soft Drinks: 79(LC); C&A: 57(TL); Camera Press/Richard Stonehouse: 52(R); Chris Fairclough Colour Library: 62(BL); Christian Dior: 21(LC); Citizen Watch (UK) Ltd: 70(BR); Cooperative Bank: 122(BC); Daimler Chrysler: 20(TR); DHL International Ltd: 14(BC), 15; Dr Marten: 49(CT); Dyson: 73(BR), 73(BR), 73(TL); EMI: 14(BR), 15, 55, 147; Express Newspapers: 95, 124(TR); Financial Times: 18(C); Ford: 40(TR), (BR), 55(C); Goodmans: 70(BR); The Guardian: 56(RB), 60(CT); HMV: 52(RC), (BL); IKEA: 5, 62(LC), (RC), (TR); Image Select International: 21(RC), 35(BC), 47(C), 47(LC), 81(TR); Image Bank: 83(RC); Inland Revenue: 85(C); Jyske Bank: 112(C); Kobal: 49(LC); Kwik-Fit: 11(RC); Lindt: 63(BL); Louis Vuitton: 21(LC), (CC), (RC); Marks & Spencer: Company Archive: 46(TR), 55; McDonald's: 15; Min Cooper: 91, 92; Modus Publicity: 71(L no.1); Molyneux Associates: 10(TR); Muji: 71(L no.2); Nordica: 22(TL); Oxfam: 130(whole page); Phillips: 107(TL); Pictor: 6(TR), 70(BR), 121(TL); Photonica: 85(LC); Pearson Education/Gareth Boden: 6(TL), 8(TL), 14(BL), 24(TR), 24(TR), 57(BL), 71(L), 72(BR), 72(BC), 107(TL), 126(TR), 128, 135(C); The Queen's Award Office: 47(TL); Reuters Ltd: 14(BC), 15; REX: 4(TR), 36(BR), 37(BL); Sony: 20(TR), 24(C); Spectrum Colour Library: 26(TL), 53(TL), 72(BL), 72(BL), 72(BR); Stock Market: 30(TC); Telegraph Colour Library: 14(TR), 26(BL), 70(TR), 132(TR); The Chase Creative Consultants Ltd: 122(BL 1,2,3&4); Time: 148(TL); Tony Stone: 10(ML), 13(TR), 17(BR), 17(BL), 26(TL), 29(BC), 36(TR), 38(TC), 43(TC), 54(TL), 56(TR), 70(BL), 79(BR), 82(TR), 84(BR), 84(BR), 84(BR), 87(TR), 108(TR), 120(TR), 120(BR), 121(TR), 121(TL), 141(TR), 143(TL), (MC), (TR); United Colors of Benetton: 20(TL); Vauxhall: 100(BL); Vidal Sassoon: 107(TL); VIATV Videophones: 80(TR); Virgin: 20(TL),

Every effort has been made to trace the holders of the copyright material and photography, but if any omissions can be rectified, the publishers will be pleased to make the necessary arrangements.

Picture research by Image Select International (London)